Essays
after a Dictionary

Also by John Vinton:

Dictionary of Contemporary Music (editor)
Diary of Light

Essays after a Dictionary

Music and Culture at the Close of Western Civilization

John Vinton

Lewisburg
Bucknell University Press
London: Associated University Presses

©1977 by Associated University Presses, Inc.

Associated University Presses, Inc.
Cranbury, New Jersey 08512

Associated University Presses
Magdalen House
136-148 Tooley Street
London SE1 2TT, England

Library of Congress Cataloging in Publication Data

Vinton, John.
    Essays after a dictionary.

    Includes bibliographical references.
    1. Music--Addresses, essays, lecture. I. Title.
ML60.V56   780'.8   76-765
ISBN 0-8387-1898-1

PRINTED IN THE UNITED STATES OF AMERICA

Contents

Acknowledgments

I would like to thank Virgil Thomson for his permission to reprint fourteen of his columns and reviews that appeared in the *New York Herald Tribune* during 1940 to 1943. I also thank Mrs. John C. Long and her brothers for their permission to reprint several memoranda written by their father, Geoffrey Parsons, to Virgil Thomson.

I am also grateful to Hans Åstrand for his permission to reprint my article "Reassessing History: Music in the United States of America," which was published in Swedish as "United States *(Förenta staterna),*" in *Sohlmans Musiklexicon* (Fall 1976).

Essays
after a Dictionary

Introduction

As the title implies, this book is an aftermath of the *Dictionary of Contemporary Music* (New York and London, 1974), for which I prepared the manuscript during 1968-1971. That project was the most profound educational experience I have had. It gave me the opportunity to recruit a "faculty" of some 200 specialists in contemporary music plus 800 or so assistants and to ask each of them to tell me what he or she knew best. The results of our collaboration are available to others, but the greatest reward remains mine alone—the opportunity I had to ask questions and to have misunderstandings identified. The essays printed here, which I prepared during 1972-1975, are a record of my attempts to absorb that experience.

Chronologically, the first of them is "The Art of Gentlemanly Discourse: Geoffrey Parsons to Virgil Thomson." Thomson was one of the advisers for my dictionary. Late in 1971 he asked me to help organize his correspondence files for transfer to the New York University Libraries. Being as meticulous in his personal habits as he is in his writing, he had left little for me to do except read the materials. Toward the end of our time together I discovered the memos that form the core of the essay.

Second in chronological order is "Restructuring Education: The Contemporary Music Project." Shortly after I finished my work with Thomson I was commissioned to write a report about CMP's accomplishments in the field of college curriculum reform. CMP, which had been founded in 1959, was about to conclude its life, and it was thought that a publication should be issued summarizing its work. Robert Werner, director of CMP and author of the "Education for the Nonprofessional" article in my dictionary, his associate David Willoughby, and I went over various papers from CMP conferences and workshops to find suitable material for an anthology. However, everything we looked at spoke more of hopes than accomplishments, and I suggested that a description of work in progress would be more forceful. It could be based on interviews with people who were using CMP ideas in their respective universities. We agreed on this approach, but the final publication never materialized.

Next came "Reassessing History: Music in the United States." *Sohlmans Musiklexikon,* the Swedish music encyclopedia, was being revised, and its editor, Hans Åstrand, asked me to write the article on American music. At first I was reluctant. Articles like this are dull to write and dull to read. But as I thought about Åstrand's proposal, I realized that he was giving me the opportunity to work out an idea derived in part from the dictionary and in part from CMP: Most of the world is just now learning what cultural multiplicity is like as a day-by-day condition of life. In the Americas, however, people have been living with multiplicity for two and three hundred years. I suspect that this aspect of our consciousness is partly responsible for the vitality that other countries find in the work being done throughout the New World. In contrast to this dynamism, however, the usual picture of U.S. music shows us as a crude, then naive population aping Europeans until somehow we equal them. Africans, Asians, Southern and Eastern Europeans, hillbillies, cowboys, these and other vigorous populations are mostly ignored in favor of the supposedly mainstream (upper-class British and French) culture of the country. I thought it would be interesting to see if and how this narrowness in our self image could be overcome. I also thought it would be worthwhile if, for once, our story began at the beginning, with the Indians, instead of later on with the Pilgrims. (A few weeks later I learned that Robert Stevenson had expressed the same idea two years before.[1])

The chief problem for me in the essay, aside from the space limitation, was my almost total ignorance of the neglected social strata and musical repertories I wanted to cover. Furthermore, no conceptual framework existed that I might follow in tying everything together. Perhaps other people more knowledgeable that I will do the more comprehensive job that is needed.

The next essay I wrote is not included here because it was superseded by "A Change of Mind." It was called "The New Values in Music" and was commissioned by Martin Goldman, editor of *Intellectual Digest*. Goldman told me he disliked most new music. He didn't say it in so many words, but what he wanted to know was the aesthetics that underlie this music. I had wanted such an article for the dictionary but no one would write it. As Goldman and I talked, I realized why: The basic information had never been brought together so that one person could comprehend it and draw conclusions. But now the consolidation had been made, and it was lying in galleys on my desk. So I went to work.

I began by rereading the major articles in the dictionary and making note of the deepest general principles they dealt with. My chief problem was learning how to identify and interpret such information. I found that to do so I had to look into

1. Robert Stevenson, *Philosophies of American Music Histories* (Washington: Library of Congress, 1970).

my own experience of music, of art, and even of life. I had to
become aware of the assumptions I had grown up with as a
child of Midwest suburban culture so that I could become
aware of alternatives and thereby assess the aesthetic choices
that contemporary composers were making. Although I had
the entire dictionary to help me and although the article I
wrote was less than 4,000 words long, it took two months of
almost daily work to put it together. The *Digest* folded before
the article could be published, and I mention the episode only
because, without the impetus it provided, I could not have
written the culminating essay, "A Change of Mind."

While "New Values" was underway, I took time out to
compile the checklist given in "A Remembrance of Things
Past: The Concerto for Orchestra." I had been keeping notes
on this genre for about three years, ever since I first noticed
how many examples exist. (Previously I had known only of
Bartók's.) I expected that compiling the list would be a routine
job, but the more I thought about the concerto for orchestra as
a genre, the more remarkable it became for me. In some ways
it epitomizes the dominant consciousness of a generation.

Now that I look back I realize that the essays thus far were
largely a preparation for "A Change of Mind." It began as a
question to myself: What distinguishes "contemporary" music?
I thought I might find an answer if I divided the stylistic features of post-1950 music into three categories—those inherited
from the nineteenth century, those that appeared in the first
half of this century, and those that have appeared since 1950.
The scheme was neat, but it would not work. After weeks of
trying to fit the facts into my three columns, I was forced to
admit that nothing fundamentally new had happened since
1950. Then I was forced to admit that although there were a
number of new ideas in the first half of the twentieth century,
these too had roots in the preceding era. It may be true that all
history is a continuum, but I was convinced that something

radically new was involved in contemporary music. Most of the dictionary's authors had indicated this to me, and they were not working in collusion. Most of them do not even know each other. What, then, was going on? I tried other ways of categorizing the information, but these too failed to satisfy me. It was a discouraging period. I was wasting my time if all I could do was substitute an inconclusive view of recent music for the frazzled patchwork that already existed.

One morning I decided to follow a hunch and treat the history of contemporary music as a process of radical change that began in the nineteenth century and reached a point of no return in the 1950s. Once I had accepted this idea I realized that many political, social, and science historians were saying the same thing about events in their fields. Finally I saw it. The evidence was everywhere. For the last century and a half Western civilization had been going out of existence, and concert music provided a firsthand account of the process as it was taking place.

The last two items, chronologically, are *"The Dictionary of Contemporary Music*: A Post Mortem" and "American Orchestral Music in Perspective." In both of them, the insights I had gained were applied to specific tasks — evaluating my dictionary and assessing the status and future of orchestral music.

May 1975

The Dictionary of Contemporary Music: A Post Mortem

All of us here look upon dictionaries and encyclopedias somewhat the way we look upon gasoline and sugar—they've become
staples of life. It hasn't always been that way, though. The
current vogue of reference books is something that has developed
only during the last hundred years.

It intrigues me why that is. What does the existence of so
many reference books in so many fields say about us as people?
I'd like to look at that question with you for a moment and
then go on to evaluate my own book in terms of where it fits
into the overall patterns I see, and where it succeeds and fails
in its approach to contemporary problems. In doing this I
think I can help you understand the modern-day challenges
that face the editor of a dictionary—any dictionary.

Obviously, we have so many reference books because
there's a lot of information around that we value and want to

A talk given in San Juan, P.R., on February 5, 1975, for The Music Library
Association, Susan T. Sommer, Program Chairperson.

17

keep track of. This raises two questions in my mind: *Why is there so much information around?* and *Why do we value it?* Perhaps these questions sound simple-minded to you. They attract me because I am interested above all else in the nature of contemporary life, and these questions don't apply to any other time or place.

The first one — Why is there so much information around? — has parallels in every field of thought and most certainly in the arts. The trend began in the early nineteenth century when the industrial revolution took hold in Europe and the Americas. This brought into existence wealth and leisure on a scale never before imagined. Today, for example, if you were to divide up the energy consumed in the United States among all the people who live here, each of us has the equivalent of 85 slaves.

During the last century and a half, as people have been acquiring all this wealth, leisure, security, and comfort, they have tended to look inward. We don't usually think of it that way, but it's true. People have tended to become aware of themselves as unique individuals. They have tended to nurture their individuality. They have tended to pursue interests that derive from their own uniqueness. People from another culture might have reacted differently, but in the West this is what happened.

Thus in the arts the concept has come to the fore that art should be self-expression. Today we take that for granted, but keep in mind that it's a recent idea. In fact it is one of the characteristics that distinguishes contemporary art from all other art.

People of a scholarly bent have been doing as artists have: They have been discovering a variety of increasingly specialized fields, fields that satisfy a variety of their own inner needs. They have gone out and uncovered information in those fields. They have themselves generated information by writing things that get listed in bibliographies and have to be memorized by graduate students—who, in turn, go out and discover and generate more new information. The wealth and technology at our disposal make it economically feasible to publish all this, and so on and on it goes. If I'm not mistaken, during the last few years the reference shelves at Lincoln Center have expanded not only to the right and left of the reference desk, but into the room behind as well.

You can take heart, though, those of you who have to buy all these books. I suspect that during the next decade the momentum will slacken considerably, and not just because of less favorable economic conditions. If you examine the new books and articles that cross your desk, you'll see that more and more of them are about things of less and less consequence— and I mean that irrespective of how well organized and foot-noted the materials may be. However pleasurable these books are for the people who write them, there are inevitably limits to what society at large will support.

The other question I asked—Why do we value all this in-formation?—is not so easy for me to answer. I've already hinted at one of the ironies involved: I don't think "we" do value it, "we" in the sense of a community, nation, society, or culture. What happens is that *some* of us value *some* information. Again, what each of us values is determined not so much by the people around us as by our own unique needs and pleasures. Remem-ber the saying a few years back, "You are what you eat"? It could just as well have been, "You are what you look up."

I am very much aware that I, as an individual, don't really value most of the information that's available to me. I've for-gotten almost everything I learned during ten years of college. I read very little. I gave up newspapers some years ago. I hardly ever accept circulars on the street.

(Let me say, however, that I always read *Notes.*[1] I'm not

1. The journal of The Music Library Association.

saying this just to flatter you. It's true. *Notes* is the only musical journal I always read.)

I'm probably an extreme case, but I think it's true of us all that no matter how much we may value the *idea* of more information, we all have defenses against it.

One other thing strikes me about our attitudes toward information. We tend to think that more is better—the more information we have, the better off we will be. But if you look below the surface, you find that it's like everything else: You gain something, you lose something. Ironically, what we seem to have lost is confidence. We have lost the confidence our ancestors had that what they knew mattered. If you think about all the things that make for a satisfying human life, we pay dearly for what we know.

Some of you probably have friends who are, today, compiling a reference book. I think I can tell you, against the general background I've outlined, what sort of problems they're facing.

One of the first questions your editor-friend must consider is, For whom is the book intended? There's a mob of people out there, more than have ever lived before. They're all pursuing their own interests in their own ways. Which of these people is an editor in the 1970s going to aim for?

I can tell you what I did, but first I want to point out that I'm speaking entirely after the fact. I was much too naive when I did my book to ask such a basic question. Instead, what I did was what almost everyone does. I drew on my own personal experience. I had been a performer, a researcher, a graduate student, a librarian, and a newspaperman. So that's what I compiled my book for—someone who had been a performer, a librarian, a researcher, a graduate student, and a newspaperman. In other words, I compiled the book for myself. And do you know what? I dearly love my book. It's the only book I've ever owned that answers the questions *I* ask. If my book is also useful to others, I think we can chalk it up largely to good luck, to the fact that someone was put in charge who had not specialized in one type of work but who had inside knowledge in several fields.

I did, however, make one conscious decision about the readers I was aiming for. They would be alive in the decade of the 70s. I figured that my book would have an active life of no more than ten years, after which it would become a rare book. Looking back, I think that's a good question for an editor to put to himself. The probable life span of his book may be the only question he can answer with confidence.

Another question an editor today must think about is, What types of information will be emphasized? Even in the narrowest of fields you've got to make choices. In my own case I found out three or four times as many things as I printed.

As I have already mentioned, my choices were based on what I wanted to know, which was, What is new and different about our time? So, in the preliminary correspondence I had with my writers, I hammered away at that question, What is unique about our time? Naturally I tried to find writers who would have a contemporary point of view—for example, Henry Brant on orchestration, Charles Wuorinen and Frederic Rzewski on performance, Hugo Weisgall on opera, Arnold Broido on publishing, and so on.

Some topics I had to think a lot about—for example, *Form.* What kind of person do you think would be most likely to have a contemporary point of view on the subject of form? I decided that it had to be a composer. Then I decided I wanted a composer who works in the most contemporary medium we have, namely electronic music. It took awhile, but I finally found James Tenney. His article on form is tough reading. Maybe it's tougher than it needs to be. But anyone who reads it carefully is going to learn things about the contemporary attitude toward form that are not explained anywhere else. I've found that the general principles Tenney outlines are applicable not just to new music but to new dance, film, and theater as well.

In some cases, to answer the question about what is unique in our time, I invented topics. One of them was *Asian Music and Western Composition,* which the composer Chou Wen-chung wrote about. Another topic was the influence of dance on music in this century. That influence has been widely acknowledged but never before investigated in detail. (One of the authors of the *Dance* article, Alan Kriegsman, has since won a Pulitzer Prize for his writings.) And perhaps most important of all, the topic *Texture.* The compositional concept, primacy of sound, is one of the characteristics that distinguishes contemporary music from all other music. Critics and academics have been fighting it tooth and nail for almost a century, but its rise has been inexorable, even within the context of 12-tone and serial music. That's what the article on texture is about. The topic turned out to be too much for one person, so I got two, both of them composers, Paul Lansky and Malcolm Goldstein. "I don't want a harangue," I told them, "I want a description." What they gave me is the first detailed analysis that anyone has attempted.

I've said a lot just now about my own influence on the dictionary, but I would have to say to our 1970s editor that the most dangerous thing he could do would be to rely solely on his own judgment. There are overall things like consistency of style, perspective, and proportion that an editor should keep his eye on, but I think it's essential, first to get good people to help you, and second to trust them.

Again I'm speaking after the fact. It's something I realized only after the book was finished. At the time I was working on it my perception was simply: These writers are working hard, harder than I ever would have imagined, and I'm learning a lot from them. My chief demand was that I, personally, understand everything that got printed. And of course that's a double demand. It involved myself as well as my writers.

I'd like to spend the rest of my time here on the subject of where I think my book fails. It's not that I enjoy being negative, but rather that we can learn a great deal from our mistakes. I think it's the only way I've ever learned anything.

Everything I've said so far has touched on one central issue: multiplicity. This is one of the basic facts of life in our time, and it's one of the basic facts of art. We expect artists to do radically different things from each other. From composers we don't want just a new tune but a whole new system of music. (Like almost everything else that's characteristic of our time, the origins of this idea can be traced back to the early nineteenth century.)

In seeking advice and help from a wide variety of people, and in trusting them, I think that I and my predecessor in the project, Eric Salzman, faced the challenge of multiplicity head-on. It was our concern that every article be written by someone who was sympathetic to the subject. (As it turned out, many of the articles on living composers were written by friends of the composer.) There too I think we faced the problem of multiplicity head-on. We also wanted to analyze contemporary developments from many different points of view. This resulted in about three-dozen large articles. Some, of course, are better than others, but I think the basic approach to the subject of contemporary music was again sound.

However, I did not adequately solve the problem of selecting composers to be given separate entries of their own, and I did not adequately solve the problem of selecting terms to be defined. In both cases the basic problem was multiplicity, but the reasons for the failure were different.

First, let me say what I did do.

As far as composers were concerned, I gathered all the information I could about all the people I could find out about.

As I remember, we began by going through a recent Schwann catalogue[2] and making 3x5 cards for every twentieth-century name there. We went through Baker's[3] and did the same thing. When there was a duplication, we simply noted the new source on the original card. I went through journals like *Notes, Perspectives of New Music, Musical Quarterly, Melos,* and *Fontes,* adding all the twentieth-century names I found in reviews and in notices of performances and new publications. I skimmed every book on contemporary music published in the 1960s and every survey article on activities within particular countries. I also took note of the people my own writers were referring to and of the recommendations of my advisory board. Eventually the card file contained 8,000 names, from which I selected 1,000 for the dictionary.

I made choices on a pragmatic basis: Who is in the news? Who is referred to the most times? Who is a U.S. reader most likely to be curious about? That's not always a question of quality, of course. It's often a matter of publicity. Since I also believe that genuine quality does eventually come to light, if some writer expressed a strong conviction that an otherwise unknown composer deserved to emerge from obscurity, and probably would within the next decade, I was inclined to include that person.

Perhaps the process could have been further refined. I don't know. I think, though, that the attempt was conscientious. So what went wrong?

Well, in the years since I finished that book I've been coming across more and more and more new names. In the U.S. alone I've become aware of a great many composers who have strong local reputations, whose music gives great pleasure to the people around them. I now realize that this is true every-

2. The *Schwann Record & Tape Guide* (Boston: W. Schwann, Inc.).

3. *Baker's Biographical Dictionary of Musicians,* 5th ed. with 1965 Supplement (New York: G. Shirmer, 1965).

where in the world. There aren't 8,000 composers who qualify for a book like mine. The number is closer to 25,000.

Like dictionaries themselves, this enormous number of composers has resulted from the increase in wealth and leisure during the last century and a half, not to mention the increase in population. And not only those things. The freedom now to do in the arts whatever you want to do encourages more and more people to be creative. That's one function of the contemporary aesthetic principle of multiplicity.

Now let me say that the composers who are included in my book *are* there, and they were all given as much attention as possible. My point is that the book could be three or four times bigger than it already is and still, in my opinion, it would not adequately reflect the situation that exists in the world today.

That was largely a physical problem. There were practical limits to how big the book could be. The matter of terms, however, was a conceptual failing. The problem was inside my own head. In the introduction to my book I stated the policy this way:

> The selection of terms to be defined was based on current usage in the U.S. and is restricted to terms that are new or have new meanings in this century. Private jargon that has not found wide acceptance is not included.

The key terms there are *private jargon* and *wide acceptance.* Private to whom? How wide? How many people have to find a word useful in order for that word to become public? If multiplicity is the central aesthetic concept of our age, then it doesn't matter how many people use a particular word. It is *the* word for *the* idea that *they* are trying to get across.

I'd like to take this one step further, which is into something I learned about myself and about my own attitude toward words. I think that basically I'm a writer. I feel most alive when

I'm at a desk working with words. That's when I lose all sense of time. I would have thought that with so much practice, words would be the things I would be most adventurous with. Sometimes that's true, but mostly, I discover, using words is where I'm most conservative. I'm not a composer or a choreographer or a filmmaker, and I'm constantly dazzled by all the things that turn up in those fields. There I really do love multiplicity. But not when it comes to words. The things closest to home are the things I'm most uptight about. I think of that as my quarter-million-dollar insight, because that's how much it cost to produce the dictionary.

Again, let me add that the terms that are in my book *are* there, and they were all handled as carefully as possible. But the policy for selecting them was based on a past conception of art and life and not on the present state of things.

As far as our 1970s editor is concerned, the part that multiplicity plays in his own work will be less severe if he is working in a pre-nineteenth-century period. It will increase in severity as he gets closer to our own day. But even in dealing with subjects from the past, today's editor will come across serious conflicts about the limits of the field, about terminology, about the questions that should be asked, about the meaning of facts—in other words, about the basic underlying structure of thinking in the field.

It's hard to talk about things at this deep a level, but I hope you understand that I'm referring to something much deeper than a mere difference of opinion. When you and your colleagues share a common culture, then you can have a difference of opinion. You can express your differences intelligibly to each other, and you can probably find a resolution. But when you don't share a common cultuare, which is one of the aspects of multiplicity, then the differences between you are likely to be radical. They are likely to involve the underlying structure of your being. As far as I can tell, most of the big mistakes these days are made because people don't realize how radical our differences and our problems really are.

I came here wanting very much to tell our 1970s editor how to avoid or solve the problems I became aware of after doing my own book. I tried. I even asked some of my critics for advice. Apparently that's a good way to get them off your back.

So here's what little I've come up with on my own. It's not a solution. It's just some rudimentary advice. And frankly, it's not very original. You've all heard similar things before.

1) Don't trust anything they told you in school. 2) Ask everyone you know to help you. If you have to, get down on your knees and beg them. 3) Trust those people. 4) Don't think you'll be definitive. Definitive books went out about 1911. 5) When it's all over, go away someplace — Puerto Rico maybe. Think about what you've been doing. Don't stop thinking until you've uncovered at least two basic misconceptions in your approach.

Then, if anyone will listen to you, tell them what you've learned.

December 1974 - January 1975

The Art of
Gentlemanly Discourse:
Geoffrey Parsons to
Virgil Thomson

Virgil Thomson was no upstart music critic when, on October 10, 1940, he joined the *New York Herald Tribune*. He was 43 years old and already well-known as a composer and critic and as an intimate of famous actors, artists, novelists, composers, and playwrights. Dozens of his music and book reviews had already appeared in *Vogue, Vanity Fair, The American Mercury, The New Republic,* and *Modern Music,* and his first book, *The State of Music,* had been published in 1930. Still, he was not quite the Thomson we revere today, the critic whose daily reviews and Sunday columns are being reread and reprinted 30 years after they first appeared. The difference, as Thomson acknowledges, was his mentor at the *Tribune,* Geoffrey Parsons (1879-1956).

Parsons was chief editorial writer for the paper and overseer of the cultural departments. He had taken on these jobs during the 17-year tenure of Thomson's predecessor, Lawrence

Gilman, a man whose style and manner epitomized the cultivated taste of his day. Parsons was responsible for hiring Thomson, and he was "committed to making a success" of his new critic.[1] He knew that Thomson had a quick mind and interesting insights and that he was in tune with vital currents of the day. But he also realized that his protégé needed taming when it came to daily journalism. "Sometimes," he wrote on May 2, 1941, "I almost despair of your ever becoming a newspaper writer." Parsons not only spoke his mind on this matter but wrote it, and his memoranda to Thomson are among the sharpest lessons in newspaper reviewing I know. They are, in addition, lessons in fine editing, for in pleading with Thomson to be precise, courteous, and generous, Parsons was merely asking that Thomson affirm the best of his innate qualities. When, according to his memo of November 29, 1940, Parsons's friends spoke of "the new Virgil," Parsons could rightly say (and doubtless with pride), "I explained that there was only one of you."

I am grateful to Parsons's sons and daughter for allowing me to publish their father's memos. I am also grateful to Thomson not only for providing me the opportunity to study this material, but for his permission to reprint the "blunders" (to use Parsons's term) and the "peaches and cream" to which Parsons's memos refer.

I

V.T.: Review of October 11, 1940

Age Without Honor
PHILHARMONIC-SYMPHONY ORCHESTRA, John Barbirolli, conductor, opening concert of the season last night in Carnegie Hall with the following program.

1. Virgil Thomson, *Virgil Thomson* (New York: A. A. Knopf, 1966), p. 331.

Overture to "Egmont"	Beethoven
Enigma Variations	Elgar
Symphony No. 2 in D major	Sibelius

The Philharmonic-Symphony Society of New York opened its ninety-ninth season last evening in Carnegie Hall. There was little that could be called festive about the occasion. The menu was routine, the playing ditto.

Beethoven's overture to "Egmont" is a classic hors d'oeuvre. Nobody's digestion was ever spoiled by it and no late comer has ever lost much by missing it. It was preceded, as is the custom nowadays, by our National Anthem, gulped down standing, like a cocktail. I seem to remember that in 1917 and 1918 a sonorous arrangement of "The Star-Bangled Banner," by Walter Damrosch, was current at these concerts. After so long a time I couldn't be sure whether that was the orchestration used last night. I rather think not. Last night's version seemed to have more weight than brilliance. It had the somber and spiritless sonority of the German military bands one hears in France these days. That somberness is due, I think, to an attempt to express authority through mere weighty blowing and sawing in the middle and lower ranges of the various orchestral instruments, rather than by the more classic method of placing every instrument in its most brilliant and grateful register in order to achieve the maximum of carrying power and of richness. I may be wrong about the reasons for it, but I think I am right about the general effect, unless my seat was in an acoustical dead spot of the hall, which I do not think it was. The anthem, to me, sounded logy and coarse; it lacked the buoyancy and the sweep that are its finest musical qualities.

Elgar's "Enigma" Variations are an academic effort not at all lacking in musical charm. I call them academic because I think the composer's interest in the musical devices he was employing was greater than his effort toward a direct and forceful expression of anything in particular. Like most English composers, Elgar orchestrates accurately and competently. Now, when a man can do anything accurately and competently he is always on the lookout for occasions to do that thing. In the Continental tradition of music writing, orchestration is always incidental to expression, to construction, to rhetoric. Many of the greatest composers, Chopin and Schumann, for instance, never bothered to become skillful at it in any major way. Others, like Beethoven and Brahms, always kept its fanciness down to the strict minimum of what expression needs. I've an idea Mr. Elgar's Variations are mostly a pretext for orchestration, a pretty pretext and a graceful one, not without charm and a modicum of sincerity, but a pretext for fancy work, all the same, for that massively frivolous patchwork in pastel shades of which one sees such quantities in any intellectual British suburban dwelling.

Twenty years' residence on the European continent has largely spared me Sibelius. Last night's Second Symphony was my first in quite some years. I found it vulgar, self-indulgent and provincial beyond all description. I realize that there are sincere Sibelius lovers in the world, though I must say I've never met one among educated professional musicians. I realize also that this work has a kind of popular power unusual in symphonic literature. Even Wagner scarcely goes over so big on the radio. That populace-pleasing power is not unlike the power of a Hollywood Class A picture. Sibelius is in no sense a naif; he is merely provincial. Let me leave it at that for the present. Perhaps, if I have to hear much more of him, I'll sit down one day with the scores and really find out what is in them. Last night's experience of one was not much of a temptation, however, to read or sit through many more.

The concert, as a whole, in fact, both as to program and as to playing was anything but a memorable experience. The music itself was soggy, the playing dull and brutal. As a friend remarked who had never been to one of these concerts before, "I understand now why the Philharmonic is not a part of New York's intellectual life."

V.T.: Review of October 12, 1940

Sonorous Splendors

BOSTON SYMPHONY ORCHESTRA, Serge Koussevitzky, conductor, first concert of the season yesterday afternoon

in Symphony Hall, Boston, with the following program:
A London Symphony   Vaughan Williams
Symphony No. 5, in C minor   Beethoven

BOSTON, Oct. 11—And so, in cerulean sunshine and through indescribable splendors of autumnal leafage, to Boston—the Hub of the Universe, the home of the Bean and the Cod. The home, as well, of the Boston Symphony Orchestra, the finest by all-around criteria of our resident instrumental foundations.

The sixtieth season of its concerts opened this afternoon with Vaughan Williams's "London Symphony." I remember hearing the work nearly twenty years ago in that same Symphony Hall, Pierre Monteux conducting. It is the same piece it was then, too, in spite of some cuts operated by the composer. The first two movements are long, episodic, disjointed. The third is short, delicate, neatly sequential, compact, efficacious, charming. The finale is rich and varied. Its musical material is of high quality, its instrumental organization ample and solid. Also, it is not without expressive power. Perhaps one is accustomed to the lengthiness and the slow reflective atmosphere of the symphony by the time one gets to this movement. The improvement in melodic material that manifests itself as the work progresses helps, too. In any case the last two of the symphony's four movements are anything but dull, which the first two are, and more than a little.

Making a program out of only that and Beethoven, out of one live Englishman and one dead German, classic and great though he be, is an obvious reference to current events and sympathies. The reference might have turned out in its effect to be not nearly so gracious as in its intention, had those last two movements of the "London Symphony" not been in themselves so impressive, the finale so moving and deeply somber. It was written in 1913, I believe. It might have been written last month, so actual is its expressive content.

The Vaughan Williams symphony served also as a vehicle for a display of orchestral virtuosity on the part of Dr. Koussevitzky and his men such as few orchestras are capable of offering their subscribers. Not that the piece itself is of any great difficulty; it is only reasonably hard to play, I imagine, but the Boston organization is in such a fine fettle after its Berkshire season that every passage, any passage, no matter what, serves as a pretext for those constant miracles of precision and of exact equilibrium that a first-class modern orchestra is capable of.

Musically considered, these refinements are more of a delight in themselves than a help of any kind to the work played. They rather tend, especially in the fine moulding and rounding off of phrases, to interrupt the music's continuity, to give it an exaggerated emphasis all over that tends to obliterate any real emphasis or meaning that the score may imply. Only the toughest of the classics and the most glittery of the moderns can satisfactorily resist that kind of polish in execution.

The Beethoven Fifth Symphony resists it quite satisfactorily, indeed. Dr. Koussevitzky, be it said to his credit, doesn't try to get away with too much careful modeling, either. Rather he puts his effort into a rhythmic exactitude that adds to Beethoven's dynamism a kind of monumental weight that is appropriate and good. When he tries to achieve more of that weight by forcing the strings beyond their optimum sonority, the result is not so good. The sound that comes out is less loud and less weighty than that which would have come out if the point of maximum resonance had not been surpassed.

All instrumentalists know this and conductors, of course, know too when they are calm enough to remember it. But at the back of every conductor's mind is a desire to make his orchestra produce a louder noise than any one else's orchestra can produce, a really majestic noise, a Niagara Falls of sound. Sometimes in the course of nearly every concert this desire overpowers him. You can tell when it is coming on by the way he goes into a brief convulsion at that point. The convulsion is useful to the conductor, because it prevents his hearing what the orchestra really sounds like while his fit is on. But if you watch carefully from the house you will usually find that the sound provoked out of a group of exacerbated musicians by any gesture of the convulsive type is less accurate in pitch and less sonorous in decibels than a more objectively conducted fortissimo.

It may seem graceless on my part to mention here a fault almost no conductor is free of and imply by so doing that there is something particularly regrettable about Dr. Koussevitzky's sharing it. I do mean to imply exactly that, however, because somewhere, some time, some conductor must get around to doing some serious work on the orchestral fortissimo comparable to the work that has already produced from our orchestras such delights of delicacy. And I think it not unfair to suggest that perhaps our finest instrumental ensembles might be just the groups to profit most by such an effort; that maybe it is even their duty to do something about correcting the inefficiency that comes from being overstrenuous.

G.P.: Memo of October 14, 1940

Dear Virgil:

Your Boston review was such peaches and cream from every point of view that I hesitate to revert to the Philharmonic piece at all. You struck the exactly right note in Boston—of wise, modest, generous, urbane, constructive comment—and I'm not worrying about the future. But having jotted down these notes, chiefly for my own clarification, I hand them on to you as written on Friday.

Yours faithfully,
[signed] Geoffrey

Notes on the Almost Perfect Critic

1. The first principle of newspaper criticism has long been, "Never criticize an audience." I don't know just where the ancient saw came from. But I feel sure it is sound as sound—in 999 cases out of a 1,000. Perhaps the reason is about the same as that expressed in (2). The audience that a critic knocks is, after all, largely composed of the very people he

wants to have listen to him and insulting them merely makes them walk out on him.[2]

Reporting an audience's reactions is, of course, quite another matter. Whether a hall is filled or empty, whether an audience applauded or hissed or walked out is often significant news.

2. Checking up on the Philharmonic piece, I reached the conclusion that the Sibelius paragraph was the one considerable blunder in it. Added to the general abruptness of the style and the too many first personal pronouns—due to the harassment of making a deadline, I know, since your natural writing is quite other—you unintentionally committed the one cardinal sin of criticism, that of appearing to condescend.

When you cited the opinion of "musically educated" people, you made every illiterate and amateur who disagreed with you simply snort and quit. "What the hell, the experts have always been wrong in estimating the importance of creative work. Here's another cocksure wise-guy. Provincial is Sibelius? Well, then, that's what I like." And so on.

Looking backward it seems clear to me that, holding the views that you do of Sibelius, you should have reserved comment upon him until later, registering only your general attitude. For what you had time and room to say that evening was not an effective way to cope with the Sibelius cult. (In your haste you also left the reader wondering what right you had to criticize Sibelius at all since you boasted of knowing very little about him. I know that compression gave this misleading twist—but there it was.) I think you will discover very soon that the huge audience available to you in the Herald Tribune can be reasoned with endlessly but that it will resent being "told". I do not mean that you should alter in the slightest degree your

---

2. Before the October 11 review was printed, Parsons had suggested that Thomson's reference to "an undistinguished audience" be deleted.

convictions or tone down their expression. But a cult is a cult and must be approached patiently and calmly—the way you would a nervous horse, let's say. You're up against a real cult in the Sibelius people and I don't know a better job that needs to be done than its gradual persuasion to the light. But you've first got to understand the cult, its sources, etc., and make clear to its members that you understand the power of its appeal, before you can get any distance in coping with it.

Ditto about almost everything else, I guess. When you come back to the Philharmonic, for instance, now that you have thrown down your gauntlet, the real problem remains of convincing the Philharmonic supporters. It is no trick to persuade the real music lovers—they were already persuaded and had deserted the Philharmonic for the Boston and Philadelphia, from orchestra seats to gallery. Your job now is to make it clear to every subscriber who can read words of more than one syllable, that so far from being a Young Pedant in a Hurry, with a Paris condescension, you are a fair, patient judge, anxious to help. It is a great tragedy for the city that the Philharmonic should have relapsed into such stodginess. It hurts you more than it does Barbirolli. You search and search for what is good—Barbirolli did do a good job with Purcell last season, for instance,—and your anger is a nothing to your sorrow. Well, I write as an old specialist in pleading, rather than a critic. But there is the direction in which you can best build up a large reading public and do musical service, I am sure.

You'll have to get the feel of it yourself. The opportunity is utterly different from that of "Modern Music",[3] let us say. You have before you in the pews not only the educated and the partly educated, but also the illiterate, musically speaking. When you write such swell prose as the Boston piece, believe me you

3. Parsons is referring to the quarterly *Modern Music,* published by the League of Composers.

can talk also to a huge audience composed not only of music-lovers but of countless folk who are glad to know what is going on anywhere in the intellectual world, provided the tale of it is told simply and entertainingly — as you tell it.

3. I'll repeat what I think I said about nationalism last evening. It's loaded today with so much prejudice and passion that you'll have to lean over backward to avoid it. N.B. The job you did in Boston on Vaughan Williams could not have been more skillful in this regard. If I had seen it I would not have bothered to write the above.

4. I suggest that you try to check up a little on Gilman's predilections and, when disregarding them as you must, of course, unhesitatingly do whenever you disagree with them, slay them as politely as you can. He, for instance, took a great shine to Ives's work last year. I can't remember what he thought of the songs, but he was much moved by the Concord Sonata, etc. I see that there are some Ives songs on the program of the New Friends of Music next Sunday. Incidentally, I shall myself be interested to know what you think of Ives[4] — an odd sort of figure, far removed from any racket, and to my ear showing originality and force in the Concord piece. What I think is of no possible importance, as I've listened to very little modern music — but this prospective item seemed a good illustration of what I mean about Gilman — to be handled not reverently, God forbid, but courteously and generously, as I know you would mean to do if you were aware of the situation.

G.P.

4. Thomson's review on October 21, 1940, of the New Friends of Music concert contains these comments on Ives: "Charles Ives's songs have a certain sincerity and worthiness about them. On the whole they are pretty kittenish. The texts are kittenish; the accompaniments are practically kitty on the keys. Only short passages of 'Evening' and 'Charles Rutledge' have any musical or prosodic inevitability about them, and they sound more like improvisation than like organic composition. The finale of 'General Booth Enters Heaven,' however, the part built around the hymn-tune "There Is a Fountain Filled With Blood," is first-class music. The double harmonies are not just a blur, as Ives's harmonies so often are. They are like a prism that defracts, a lens that amplifies; and their notation and placing are as precise as a good job in optics."

II

Music From Chicago
Points East and West

CHICAGO SYMPHONY ORCHESTRA, Frederick Stock, conductor, concert last night at Carnegie Hall with the following program:

Overture to "Euryanthe"	Weber
Symphony No. 3, in F major	Brahms
American Creed	Roy Harris
Till Eulenspiegel	R. Strauss

Flowers on the stage and flowers in the musicians' buttonholes, two fiftieth seasons to celebrate, that of the Chicago Symphony Orchestra and that of our own Carnegie Hall, an exchange of visits between Chicago's orchestra and our own Philharmonic—what with all this and a new work by Roy Harris, last night was indeed a sufficiently festive occasion for flowers on the stage and flowers in the musicians' buttonholes.

The Chicago Symphony Orchestra sounds like a French orchestra. Its fiddle tone, thin as a wedge, espouses by resemblance that of oboe and trumpet, absorbs nothing, stands clear in the orchestral bouquet. All the instrumental sounds stand clear and separate. Their harmony is one of juxtaposition, not of absorptive domination. As in an eighteenth-century flower picture, all is distinct, nothing crushed.

Mr. Stock won his audience last night, as he has won audiences for thirty-five years, by playing them music very beautifully, not by wowing them. I missed the "Euryanthe" overture, save through a crack. The Brahms third symphony was a dream of loveliness and equilibrium. It is the best built, the most continuous of Brahms's symphonies; and it contains, on the whole, the best melodic material of the four. With no weakness of its structure to conceal and no gracelessness in its musical content to disturb the clarity of its message, it offered Mr. Stock occasion for one of those rare and blessed readings in which the music seems to play itself. Especially the end movements, the first and the last, floated on a Viennese lilt, pastoral, poetic and effortlessly convincing. The passage in the finale was particularly happy where the wind plays sustained harmonic progressions which the violins caress with almost inaudible tendrils of sound, little wiggly figures that dart like silent goldfish around a rock.

"Till Eulenspiegel" was merry, though perhaps a trifle discontinuous. Its prankiness, however, was light and gay and nearer by far to the humor of its author than those weighty readings we sometimes hear that make it sound like the ponderous pleasantries of a machine gun.

Mr. Harris's "American Creed" invites kidding, as all of his programmistically prefaced works do. If we take his music as he offers it, however, we risk refusing a quite good thing. No composer in the world, not even in Italy or Germany, makes such shameless use of patriotic feelings to advertise his personal product. One would think, to read his prefaces, that he had been awarded by God, or at least by popular vote, a monopolistic privilege of expressing our nation's deepest ideals and highest aspirations. And when the piece so advertised turns out to be mostly not very clearly orchestrated schoolish counterpoint and a quite skimpy double-fugue (neither of which has any American connotation whatsoever) one is tempted to put the whole thing down as insincere and a bad joke.

The truth, however, is other. Mr. Harris, though the bearer of no exceptional melodic gifts and the possessor of no really thorough musical schooling, has an unquenchable passion to know and to use all the procedures of musical composition. He has pondered over the medieval French melodic line and over the problem of continuous (non-repeating) melodic line and he has come by this road to understand where the crucial problem lies in America's musical coming-of-age. That problem would seem to be how shall we absorb all of European musical culture rather than merely that current in Vienna between the years of 1750 and 1850. Harris has learned by meditation and hard work that if we expect to produce music worthy to rank with that of the Viennese masters we must go through a selective evolution comparable to that which took place in Europe for at least three centuries before the miracle of Vienna occurred.

He knows that musical material, even folk-lore material, is as international as musical form and syntax, that localism is no more than one man's colorful accent. He knows this so well that he avoids, as though it were of the devil, any colorful accent whatsoever. He puts his musical effort on serious problems of material and of form. He does not always get anywhere in his music; but it is serious music, much more serious than his blurbs would lead one to believe.

He is monotonous in his material and in his form. (All his pieces begin alike.) But every now and then something really happens. It happened last night in the closing pages of both movements of his "Creed." It was unexpected, original (in spite of the Stravinsky allusion) and beautiful. And it had exactly as much to do with America as mountains or mosquitoes or childbirth have, none of which are anybody's property and none of which have any ethnic significance whatsoever.

V.T.: Review of November 25, 1940
Theater and Religion

ARTURO TOSCANINI, conducting the N. B. C. Symphony Orchestra, assisted by Zinka Milanov, soprano; Bruna Castagna, contralto; Jussi Bjoerling, tenor; Nicola Moscona, bass; and the Westminster Choir, Dr. John Finley Williamson, director, Saturday night at Carnegie Hall in a concert for the Alma Gluck Zimbalist Memorial of The Roosevelt Hospital Development Fund, with the following program of Giuseppe Verdi's music:

Te Deum, for two four-part choirs and orchestra
Requiem, composed in memory of Alessandro Manzoni, for four solo voices, chorus and orchestra.

Managers refer to him as The Maestro. Orchestral players call him The Old Man in much the same spirit of reverence and healthy fear with which persons resident on the banks of the Mississippi never use any other name for that mighty stream than simply The River. This department had anticipated employing the polite but noncommittal form, Mr. Toscanini. After last Saturday night's rendition of the Verdi Te Deum and Requiem, we feel more like shouting to the nation simply, "The Old Man is back!"

No better piece could he have chosen than the Verdi Requiem to make us appreciate his qualities as a master of musical theater. Gaudy, surprising, sumptuous, melo-dramatic and grand is Verdi's homage to Italy's poet and his own dear friend, Manzoni. No religious musical work of the last century is more sincerely or more completely what it is. Theatrical religion or religious theater? Let him answer who could tell us the same of nineteenth-century Neapolitan church architecture. Nowhere as in Naples does the eye find such constant verification of what the ear tells us when we listen to Palestrina, to Bach, to Mozart, namely that to the sincerely religious there is no difference between sacred and secular style.

Verdi, though not a particularly pious man, was a sin-cere Catholic; he was also a sincere man of the theater and a sincere Italian. His Requiem is as sincere as a piece of theatrical Italian Catholicism as has ever been written. Sin-cere Protestants often find it shocking. Sincere non-believers are likely to find it comic. But so might any one find the Dies Irae itself who had no stomach for horror.

The only sound esthetic standard I know of that covers all works and epochs is that anything is all right if it is enough so. That is to say that extremism in art, when it really is extreme, and middle-of-the-road normality, when it is really clear and comprehensible to all men, carry in their very extremism and universality the hallmarks of their authenticity. The Verdi Requiem has never raised any eyebrows in Naples (with which city, the seat of Verdi's greatest operatic successes, I like to identify it spiritually) or even in Milan (where it was first performed, in 1874). The question of its acceptance into the musical tradition of Protestant America is still, on account of its extreme theatricality, undecided.

As music that is not only very beautiful in itself, but that is also really "enough so," I give it my vote. I have not always been of that mind; I have long considered it an oddity of which the intrinsic worth scarcely justified the difficulties of a proper execution. After Saturday's performance I have no reserves.

The Maestro conducted it as if it were no more complicated that the "Miserere" from "Il Trovatore" and no less splendidly compelling than "Otello" or "La Traviata." The Westminster Choir, handsomely gowned in white satin and violet velvet of ecclesiastical cut, sang perfectly. But perfectly. The soloists, Zinka Milanov, Bruna Castagna, Jussi Bjoerling and Nicola Moscona, sang like stars from some celestial opera house. The two ladies merit each a mark of 99 per cent for their rendition of the impossible Agnus Dei passage in parallel octaves unaccompanied. The kettle-drummer, whose name I do not know, merits mention in heaven for his two-stick, unison explosions in the Dies Irae and for the evenness of his Verdian *ppppp* rolls elsewhere.

Worthy of mention, too, is the implied homage to a regretted musician in the choice of this particular program by Mr. Toscanini to raise money for the Alma Gluck Zimbalist Memorial of the Roosevelt Hospital Development Fund. Just as the great expatriate Italian could have chosen no work more advantageous for himself to conduct, I can think of no more appropriate piece of music with which to honor the memory of a much-loved opera singer than Verdi's sincerely and superbly operatic Requiem.

G.P.: *Memo of November 29, 1940*

Dear Virgil:

I hear such warm and friendly words talked about you — "the new Virgil", as one of my friends put it. I explained that there was only one of you, etc., etc. Then I got to thinking what it was that your last month's writing had that your early weeks with a hatchet, hacking your way through the musical jungles of Manhattan, didn't have. Having worked the point out in my own mind, perhaps you will let me set it down in words for your eyes and edification. It seems to me much more important than any details we have been talking of—is in fact the essential basis of all persuasive, potent criticism.

The point is not all one of the amount of praise or criticism that you dole out. It is a question of human understanding of the enormous difficulties involved in any musical composition or performance, of explaining those difficulties to the reader and of stating your criticism, however severe, in relation to this human effort. Take your piece on Harris, as an illustration. You certainly didn't leave his composition very much when you got through but you did give me my first clear notion of what the man was trying to do and what specifically was wrong with his work. I remember the bright phrase with which young Mr. Haggin[5] dismissed Harris last winter—to the effect that the music so far from evoking "the bare and windy spaces of Kansas," suggested to Haggin only "the bare and windy spaces of Harris's mind." Haggin can write with enormous swank and style; but the sweeping gesture got me not one inch forward.

The gist of my reflection, a real discovery for me, is that since readers are human beings, the best way to put across a criticism to them of an artistic achievement, is in terms of human nature. Sounds like heresy for anyone who thought he had subsisted on pure music all his life, as I had supposed. But I suspect there's a lot of truth in it.

Looking back to your earlier reviews, I think they were dry and crackly and lacked juice and life in comparison with these later ones. Neither sparkle of wit, nor the one word of apt slang, nor the justest of definitions, can hold the reader, make him believe in you, and educate him, as can sympathy, good nature, generosity, and all the other traits that go to demonstrate understanding of the human animal.

The Requiem piece was another good illustration. I think it was one of your best, both in respect to the music itself and to "The Old Man". By your Neapolitan background you some-

5. Parsons is referring to the critic B. H. Haggin.

how made me understand what was good and bad in the Requiem as I never had before. I hope you can go on with Toscanini as a conductor and by praising him discreetly, indicate his short-comings. He is the town's local hero but I know you can do the trick and get away with it.

In a different stratum, yet with very much the same local aura, is the Wagner problem. I don't know how you feel about Wagner but personally I hunger for someone to differentiate between Wagner great and Wagner merely good, or banal. Yet here is another local god. Perhaps some of the earlier idolatry has waned but Wagner's music still means an enormous something to oodles of real music lovers. I shall be waiting for the words of discriminating wisdom that the town has long lacked on the subject.

In the meantime you are turning out fine juicy stuff that everybody is reading. Good luck to you!

Yours affectionately,
[signed] Geoffrey

III

V.T.: *Review of March 24, 1941*

Renaissance, Baroque, Rococo and Late Romantic
NEW FRIENDS OF MUSIC ORCHESTRA, Fritz Stiedry, con-
ductor, concert yesterday at 5:30 in Carnegie Hall, with Yves
Tinayre, barytone, as assisting artist in the following program:

Symphony in F major, No. 67	Haydn
Sonnet de Petrarque, "Stanza alla Vergine"	Guillaume Du Fay
Motet pour Paques	Nicolas Gombert
Concertato for solo voice and nine instruments	Claudio Monteverdi
Mr. Tinayre	
Serenade for Strings	Tchaikovsky

It never got to be clear in my mind whether the program had been changed or whether I had come the wrong day. I thought there was to be a "Symphonietta" (so spelled, I assure you, in the New Friends of Music Program Book for 1940 and 1941: there has been, in fact, a slight epidemic this winter of that preposterous diminutive) a symphonietta by Roger Sessions. But when I got there, there was no mention of Roger Sessions; there were works by Haydn and Tchaikovsky and some fine pieces from the Renaissance repertory of Monsieur Yves Tinayre. In fact, all these were so eminently agreeable that I forgot to ask what had become of the Sessions. Perhaps the mistake was mine and there never has been any question of playing it today. I wonder if what is more likely, it didn't turn out to be more difficult to play than had been counted on in estimating rehearsal time.

The Haydn symphony turned out to be the second New York performance of a work of which the existence has long been known but the manuscript lacking. I believe Mr. Albert Einstein came across it several years back. It is in every respect a first-rate Haydn symphony, and Mr. Stiedry's musicians played it in the fine brilliant style that is currently accepted as the best way to play Haydn. I find that style a bit brittle. It is merry and coquettish but mostly sort of dry, as if all sentiment and depth were being reserved for Mozart. As a matter of fact, square-toed Papa Haydn is as ill-cast in the rôle of the Dresden china shepherdess as was poor starving Mozart. But it seems to be thought that some respected composer must be given the rôle that the mid-nineteenth century thought it necessary to invent in order to set off its picture of Beethoven as the Liberator of Music. Haydn might as well be so cast as any one, if the rôle must be played at all. At least, he isn't asked to simper, as Mozart used to be.

Monsieur Tinayre sings both lyrically and robustly, withal a bit nasally, as was, I believe, the vocal style considered most correct before the seventeenth century, a vast repertory of music from the late Middle Ages and the Renaissance.

The works of Du Fay and of Gombert, pupil of the great Josquin des Prés, that were performed yesterday with instrumental accompaniment are noble examples of the burning lyric intensity that was characteristic of the Flemish and somewhat of the Burgundian school in the fifteenth century. The Concertato of Monteverdi is more like the music of the great Baroque epoch that it inaugurated. It is spatially conceived for three groups of instruments. There is a string choir, an organ with cellos and bass, and (as intimate companion to the singing voice) a group of plucked instruments, presumably lutes and theorbos, yesterday represented by a modern harp.

With the exception of the organ and harp parts, which are his own realizations from the figured bass, Monsieur Tinayre assured me that all the notes executed are by Monteverdi. I asked because I was aware that no famous composer has been subject to more "restoration" than he. Especially the opera scores have been re-invented since in most cases all that exists in manuscript are the vocal parts, the figured bass and the list of instruments employed by the composer.

The Concerto is charming as well as authentic, though not nearly so sensual musically as its love-poem (anonymous) might lead one to expect. The restrained and somewhat mysterious air of the whole thing, and also the utterly fantastic nature of the poet's conceit (he tastes his Lady's lips while listening to her lovely words and wishes he could also taste her words while listening to the meaning of her kisses) makes me think it possibly a bit of that troubadour verse now considered by some to have been the secret and hermetic style through which the Manichean heresy was kept alive after the Albigensian Crusade. This, if it were true, and if we may suppose that Monteverdi knew at least enough about the true meaning of such verse to make him give to the musical declamation of it a certain restrained and almost ritual tone, would make the work more convincing to me than it would be if I were obliged to consider the whole thing as just a bit of gallant fluff.

V.T.: Review of March 31, 1941

Registering High Satisfaction
NEW FRIENDS OF MUSIC ORCHESTRA, Fritz Stiedry, conductor, first performance of Mr. Stiedry's orchestral version of Johann Sebastian Bach's "Art of Fugue," yesterday at 5:30 in Carnegie Hall. Assisting pianists, Ernst Victor Wolff and Ignace Strasfogel.

There are no questions in music more controversial than those that regard the performance possibilities of Bach's *Kunst der Fuge.* Whether it should be orchestrated at all and, if so, how; what should be done about the canons and where should they be played, if at all; not to speak of how to finish off an unfinished work—all these minor matters have always caused more argument in musical circles than the major ones that regard the articulating and phrasing of the work's melodic substance.

In the long run, most of such controversy is futile, because nothing one does to this work ever really hurts it. It is a piece that never fails to make a profound impression, a deep musical incision, so to speak, upon the mind of anybody who likes music. One would scarcely expect a work apparently so recondite, four canons and sixteen fugues on the same subject or on material derived from this, to please so universally. Yet it does. The large orchestral version by Wolfgang Graeser that was current in the 1920's was so ardently patronized in Germany, I am told, that special "Art of the Fugue" expresses were run from Berlin to Leipzig to take care of the crowds whenever it was given. Yesterday's performance of the Stiedry version filled Carnegie Hall, in spite of spring week-end weather, with an audience that listened with absorption and at the end applauded for a long time.

This reviewer, like everybody else, passed a rare and lovely hour and a half. He passed an even more satisfactory one than those persons did who take more seriously the controversial questions raised by the work. Not that he hasn't, like everybody else, his pet theories about it. It is rather that he finds himself in accord with Fritz Stiedry on many of those points—on enough of them, indeed, to make him tolerant of solutions with which he is not quite in accord with others.

The order of play, for instance, I find eminently agreeable. The interspersing of the four canons among the fugues relieves any possible monotony of these, and in addition sets off the canons themselves to great advantage. Also, the general pattern of the instrumentation, which is for small orchestra, some of the fugues being scored for only four or five instruments, pleases me more than that of the more weighty and luxuriant Graeser version. It also seemed to me that the Stiedry scoring was done with conviction, with style and with a great deal of fine musical taste.

The orchestra's coloration was lively, though at no time garish. Stiedry has avoided equally the soggy and meretricious. The essential of his scheme is a seeking after sonorities and oppositions that resemble those of eighteenth-century organs. Contrasts of timbre and neatness of articulation are sought rather than weight or mass of mere sound. He has not hesitated, however, to use mixed timbres, any more than an organist does. His sparing but effective entries for brass, for example, are made with the same considerations in mind that an organist would have in drawing the heavy reed stops. As a result, the fugues take on a grandeur that is due entirely to their shape and proportions, never to any preoccupation with the merely heroic. It would be difficult for me to express otherwise than by simply stating the fact the extreme satisfaction that I, for one, derived from listening to a work which is, in the opinion of all, one of the great summits of musical achievement, without being at any time assaulted and blackjacked by tonal or interpretative insistences.

The "Art of the Fugue" would be pleasurable to hear played by no matter whom on no matter what. Even on four harmonicas or on a Spanish guitar it would have depth and splendor. Played with such lively intelligence and such loving discernment as were employed yesterday in Stiedry's delicate and eminently sensible version, it became something long to cherish in one's memory. I should like to add also my own roses and compliments to those of the audience for the beautiful playing of the canons on two pianos by Mr. Wolff and Mr. Strasfogel.

G.P.: Memo of March 31, 1941

Dear Virgil:

Just a line to tell you how right and beautiful your review of the "Art of Fugue" seemed to me. I had been quite bowled over by the concert and seized the Herald Tribune with eagerness at 11:30, hoping that you had gone, but not knowing. I can only say that your piece moved me in much the same way that the concert did. Technically it seemed to me to have everything that the finest criticism possesses. You conveyed a picture not only of the highly technical points involved, but also what is more difficult and far rarer, a feeling of the scene. And like a first-rate newspaperman you didn't forget the two pianists, who were just as good as the orchestra in my judgment.

Let me also take advantage of this note to tell you how much I also admired the criticism of the Yves Tinayre concert.

My best, as ever.

G.P.

[signed] Geoffrey

IV

V.T.: Review of April 23, 1941

Amateur Symphony

STAMFORD SYMPHONY ORCHESTRA, John Barnett, conductor, concert Monday night in the high school auditorium at Stamford, Conn., with Percy Grainger, composer-pianist, as soloist and guest conductor in the following program:

Suite, "Imagery"   Horace Johnson
Piano Concerto in A minor   Grieg

Mr. Grainger

Ancient Desert Drone	Henry Cowell
Polka and Rondo	Field, arr. Sir Hamilton Harty
The Walk to the Paradise Garden, from "A Village	
Romeo and Juliet"	Delius
Mock Morris: Colonial Song	Grainger
Mr. Grainger conducting	
Handel in the Strand, for piano and orchestra	Grainger
Mr. Grainger	

Amateurs playing chamber music in the home often achieve a fair degree of professional finish in their execution. Even when they don't, they do a thing interesting to themselves and to casual listeners by merely reading through classic and modern repertory. Amateurs singing in chorus often achieve, in addition to these same cultural advantages, a degree of finished execution that, superposed on the amateurs' intent sincerity, gives a higher artistic result than it is commonly possible to achieve in paid groups. It has never seemed to me that amateur symphony orchestras accomplished much for anybody.

It isn't that I mind inferior execution. It is simply that orchestral music is an objective thing, and an objective thing has to be done in an objective way. Communion is not essential to it as it is to quartet playing and to choral singing, though the best results do require a certain amount of spontaneous teamwork. What is essential to orchestral playing is technical progress. An orchestra must always be getting better technically, under a given leadership, or else it gets worse. The clearer and clearer rendering to audiences of composers' intentions is its only possible goal.

Student orchestras often accomplish this admirably and so do groups of inferior professional musicians gathered together for that purpose. There is something static about the technique and the musical outlook of amateur musicians which renders them resistant to musical direction and timid about projecting a musical conception. They have lots of good will and they enjoy rehearsing. But I have rarely heard an orchestral concert by amateur executants, however skillful many of these may have been individually, which seemed to me to get over the footlights with much of the composers' original intention or even with any erroneous but forceful distortion of same.

The Stamford Symphony Society, which I heard on Monday evening, is an amateur group of sixty functioning for pleasure in a rather highly cultivated suburban community. It has been functioning for seventeen years. Its present conductor, Mr. John Barnett, is a bright young man not without skill or schooling at his trade. And yet the actual sounds the orchestra produces have small musical interest. The playing on Monday was constantly off pitch, and there was little instrumental balance of an objective kind.

The program was interesting. Mr. Horace Johnson's suite called "Imagery" is gentle music and not ungracious to the ear. Henry Cowell's "Desert Drone" is a quite skillful piece of orchestral impressionism. The Delius and the Field works are orchestral trickery far beyond the abilities of the group to execute. But Grieg and Grainger are straightforward musicians and entirely appropriate for unstable performers.

Mr. Grainger himself, though not a great pianist, is a good musician, and he has invaluable platform charm. His own works, though not profound, are buoyant and full of a muscular exuberance that never fails to lift up the spirits. His "Mock Morris" dance for strings, as he conducted it, was the evening's most gratifying moment.

I suspect that guest conductors, though they can ruin great orchestras, are the best tonic in the world for lesser groups. That is, provided the group has, as most of these lesser groups do, a regular trainer and drillmaster responsible for the orchestra's technical progress and discipline. I suspect also, however, that amateur groups like the Stamford Symphony are awfully hard for anybody to do anything with objectively and progressively.

V.T.: Sunday column of May 4, 1941
Music as Civic Virtue

Whenever reviewers from this department have gone out to the suburbs (or farther afield) to observe and report upon neighborhood musical activities, they have been greeted with enthusiasm and hospitality; and their subsequent published reviews of such activities have, naturally enough, constituted for the neighborhood in question matter for considerable dither. The pattern of that dither varies in no way from what takes place in the metropolis when civic music is criticized publicly.

Criticism is just one vote in that necessary pronouncing of judgment by the community itself and by its visitors on how worth while such efforts are. When I questioned the value of all such efforts after hearing one bad concert, I was, I admit, being a bit unfair, though I must say I have heard in the past many another amateur orchestra that seemed in my private estimate to be accomplishing little for anybody beyond providing its members with something to do on Monday evenings. But it is equally true that many such groups form hotbeds of home-grown musical life that are invaluable to the intellectual life of the community, as well as to its social solidarity.

But all that depends on each musical organization's musical behavior. No community is ennobled by doing anything in an indifferent manner. Civic efforts are fine if they come to something. If not, they render future civic efforts more and more difficult to organize. When a music critic goes to a performance at the local opera house or to a community concert and writes about it, he is neglecting both his civic and his professional duty, I should say, if he does not review the occasion in terms of its musical clarity and effectiveness, taking into account, of course, as one does, the musical pretentions and possibilities of the executants engaged in the project. Because before music, however simple, can have any cultural value in a community's life it must be musically worthy both of the persons who make it and of the public that supports it.

Certainly the value and interest of a musical performance is as much dependent on who gives it as on what it really sounds like. One demands less of professional finish from a student recitalist than from a touring concert artist. Pedagogues and composers, when they perform in public, are not necessarily competing with virtuosos on the latter's own ground of brilliant execution. Their specialty is rather the correct exposition of a piece's musical shape and substance, in so far as these are separable from brilliant execution, as in fact they more often than not are. W. P. A. musical units exist primarily for non-musical reasons; their membership is not chosen for musical accomplishment alone. Consequently, it would be absurd to expect a W. P. A. orchestra to play as well as the Philharmonic. Curiously enough, New York City's occasionally does. Youth orchestras, students' training orchestras, women's orchestras and strictly amateur groups all are forgiven in any sensible person's mind roughness of execution that would be considered highly objectionable from a highly paid professional ensemble.

This is all perfectly well understood, and everybody knows that brilliance of execution is not an essential quality of good music-making. The essential quality of good music-making is the effectiveness of communication. If A hums a tune so that B can understand it, A has made a musical communication to B. If the Peanut Center Philharmonic can play a Strauss waltz clearly enough for music-minded listeners to follow the musical lines and for everybody to be able to imagine that a waltz is going on, then the Peanut Center Philharmonic is a sound musical organization. If the instrumental balances are incomprehensible, if the pitch is constantly inaccurate, if the tempo and general rhythmic progress of the performance are halting and higglety-pigglety, then the Peanut Center Philharmonic should either change its conductor or give him more rehearsal time before trying to perform in public again.

Music is like baseball; it can be played at any level of skill by professionals or by amateurs. And nobody expects Junior, aged twelve, to be Joe di Maggio. What everybody who supports a team does expect is that the game be played according to the rules. Otherwise it is not baseball and cannot be made into a public spectacle under that name.

Amateur groups, as one might expect, vary enormously in musical quality. Also their musical achievements depend far more on the conductor's skill than those of the professional groups do. As for the civic effort angle, it is not the province of this department to judge social merit, though it is our natural prejudice as musicians to approve musical activity of every kind. I should imagine, being no specialist in civic virtue, that the value of a community effort, granted the legitimacy of its aim, could be determined by the effectiveness with which it is carried out. I doubt if the mere getting of people together in the name of civic improvement does much good unless some civic improvement is thereby accomplished. I am convinced that civic orchestras bestow cultural benefits on the communities that support them. But I am also convinced that there is a certain minimum of clarity in musical rendition below which it is not wise for such groups to give or to continue giving public performances. That level is hard to define generally but not impossible to diagnose in any given case. It is the leader's business to watch it alertly. His musical integrity is determinable, after all, not by how good a performance he can give but by how bad a one he will let by.

As I said above, music doesn't have to be slick to be good. And neither do musicians have to be completely accomplished in order to have a right to communal musical exercise. But they do have to be able to play a bit, and they have to be able to give together a clear rendition of some piece, however elementary, before it is possible for them to function effectively as anything but a practice unit. When they function as a concert-giving group, it is, I think, entirely reasonable to consider the result as concert music.

This is where a comparison with the Metropolitan Opera Company comes in. The Met is something of a civic institution and ever more of a national one; it can use large amounts of encouragement, especially financial; it has devoted and civic-minded propagandists and a loving public. But in the evenings from 8 to 12 and on Saturday afternoons it is a musico-dramatic entertainment and nothing else. That is the time when the value of the civic effort which makes it possible is tested. If its performances make musical sense, that effort is justified. If not, not. If their repertory, style and finish seem worthy to the community, all is fine. If not, improvements are needed.

G.P.: Memo of May 1, 1941

Dear Virgil:

I don't think you have pulled it off in this piece.[6] Your usual technique of making complete and handsome amends at the start and then by analysis, justifying what was right in your statement, is completely reversed here. I searched in vain for the really constructive appreciation of an amateur orchestra, good or bad, and did not come upon it until the last sentence of the next to the last paragraph. There you say, "But it is equally true that many such groups are hot-beds of home-grown musical life that are invaluable to the intellectual life of the community, as well as to its social solidarity."

It seems to me that the piece ought to be completely turned around. You ought to start off with a statement of what amateur orchestras and W.P.A. orchestras do for a community, show a complete comprehension of what you have summarized in that one sentence. Let me suggest one item which I know from experience and observation: It is the fashion in which orchestras feed chamber music. You made a very beautiful and telling contrast between orchestral music and the intimacy of chamber music in your piece on Stamford. That was swell. The point I am stressing now is that chamber music groups are very difficult to evolve, as they depend upon very subtle weightings of ability and personality. There is no way, I am sure, in which members of such groups can find one another, as good as playing together in an orchestra. There they get a chance to size each other up and organize. If you believe in amateur chamber music as you so eloquently declared in your Stamford piece, then I think you ought to believe in the amateur orchestra.

---

6. Parsons is referring to a draft of Thomson's Sunday column, which was subsequently revised and printed on May 4. As Parsons indicates at the end of his memo of May 2, he helped Thomson revise the column.

I make this one point, but there are others, such as the whole revival of skills, with the arrival of fresh teachers, etc., which follows in the wake of an orchestra.

Your critical point, that unless the orchestra is conducted up to a certain level, it can do more harm than good, seems to me entirely correct. You do well to state it, and I think you state it accurately, but it should follow, not precede, the constructive, enthusiastic side of your piece. This article is a large wet blanket for all amateur performances. In my judgment it should be exactly reversed in order and in weight of content. It should be two-thirds praise of the amateur idea and one-third insisting upon critical standards. I do wish you could twist the piece around, write it in the order and in the spirit which I have outlined. In short, as you can perceive, the whole piece strikes me as nibbling and niggling in tone, when it should be good-natured, friendly and handsome—I don't mean about the gentleman from Stamford, but about amateurs in general.

G.P.

[signed] Geoffrey

G.P.: Memo of May 2, 1941

Dear Virgil:

Sometimes I almost despair of your ever becoming a newspaper writer. The Maguire letter[7] was of relatively small importance. The essential fact was that in your review your pen and foot slipped and you wrote as follows: "It has never seemed to me that amateur symphony orchestras accomplished much for anybody." If this was the truth, then your whole expedition into the hinterland was nonsense and you should have stayed

---

7. The letter does not survive.

at home. The sentence stuck out like a sore thumb in an otherwise beautiful and accurate piece. The important thing was not Mr. Maguire, but the fact of this sentence. Anybody with a modicum of newspaper training would have seen this and said to himself, "How can I best turn this from a minus into a plus?" By seizing upon the sentence, re-defining your point of view, discoursing about the amateur idea generously, humorously, etc., you could have re-captured all the irritated people and turned a defeat into a victory.

Instead of that, you go off on an issue that is important, but, shall we say, technical. I suppose it is possible to distinguish the civic aspect of an amateur orchestra from its amateurishness, and as I said in my other memorandum, I quite agree with you that a public concert must face certain standards, variable as those standards may be. I have no quarrel with any of your statements in your piece. It is just not the piece that anybody writing from day to day for a continuing audience whose attention you must hold and whose loyalty you must not flout, would think of writing.

I can't explain your blind spot except on the theory that you still haven't any feel of your audience. It is not a few specialists or a few groups, but a very large number of thousands of literate folk, the most literate audience in the city. It is an audience and you can't neglect or slight that fact. What you should most earnestly desire is that these folk should follow you from day to day. It is precisely here that writing for a newspaper differs most essentially from writing for a magazine or for a book.

Incidentally, your piece yesterday morning opens on a note that no reporter with a six months' experience would blunder into.[8] The first thing that a newspaper man learns

8. On May 1, Thomson reviewed a "Salon Swing" pops concert at the Museum of Modern Art. The opening paragraph reads: "Real coffee there was, both before the concert and during the intermission. Real swing there was, too, as program. And real thuglike manhandling of the guests by attendants, a house specialty of the Museum of Modern Art. Let that pass. Once one had run the gauntlet of the storm-troopers, the concert itself was a pleasure. A pleasure to all, as applause and happy faces were witness."

is that his audience is not remotely interested in whether his taxicab driver was impudent or negligent or whether the usher stuck out his foot and tripped him up, or whatever. It is interested solely in his opinions of what it shared with him, to wit, the performance. The temptation of every beginning reporter is to think that a fresh cop or what not is of some moment to the public. It is not. This is not to say that any member of the staff of the New York Herald Tribune needs to take anything from anybody. There are plenty of ways of getting back at anybody who tries to get fresh with a member of our staff. Your handling of the Lawrence episode[9] was perfect in this respect. This is a mere detail and I should not dignify it by referring to it in a memorandum except as it bears on your general failure to realize what writing for a newspaper must center around.

Since you suggest it, I attach a re-ordered and somewhat shortened version of "Music as Civic Virtue." I think you will agree with me that the original article was too long. This contains all the essential parts of your piece, it seems to me, and puts the one sentence about the amateurs where they will see it, in the second paragraph. If you approve, I should certainly much prefer to see the article printed in this form.

Your letter to Maguire seems to me fine and by all means send it.

G.P.
Still affectionately
[signed] Geoffrey

9. Robert Lawrence was an assistant music critic. According to Thomson, the "episode" probably had to do with a complaint from a performer about an unfavorable review.

V

V.T.: Sunday column of May 25, 1941

Philharmonic—II

Last week this column animadverted on the desirability of the Philharmonic's turning its attention away from conductors and conducting, with all the sterile deification of the past that those involve, and on to the live musical issues of the day. I opined that in view of the Philharmonic's position as our national orchestra of the air, it is necessary that it offer its ten million listeners a vigorous musical policy rather than a parade of tailcoats visible only in Carnegie Hall. I referred also to the musical inefficiencies that have resulted from our orchestra's having had no serious, first-class regular, and more or less permanent drill master since well before 1900. And I concluded that in view of a possible change in its conductor (or in any renewal of the present conductor's contract), the governing board would serve both New York Ctiy and the whole United States best if it demanded of any prospective conductor a musical program aimed at putting the Philharmonic back on its feet musically and giving it the rôle to play in our national creative life to which its ancient prestige, its nation-wide public and its elevated budget all obligate it. Equally important is it, too, that the conductor who proposes any such program be given time and full authority to carry it out. A five-year plan, I called it on another occasion.

What would such a plan entail as program? One thing only. A placing of the Philharmonic's whole weight and prestige on the side of the creative musical forces in New York City and in the United States at large. Any other policy must end by placing it in opposition to those forces, not a pretty position nor a worthy one.

I admit that its position for forty years has largely been, when you compare it to similar organizations in Boston, in Chicago, in Philadelphia even, not to speak of Minneapolis and Detroit, one of extreme conservatism about living music. And music writing has gone on just the same. So well, indeed, that America finds herself today the center of musical creation in the Western World. The present concentration of composers here is due partly to racial and to political intolerance in Europe. It is due also to the inability just now of our own men of genius to leave these shores for others that have in the past sometimes been more friendly toward creative originality. But the sum of it all is that America is now the seat of a vigorous musical culture. The number of foreign-born musicians among the leaders of that culture is not nearly so large as the number of native citizens. This fact is interesting, though of small importance. For America itself is the dominating element in practically all music made in America, just as Austria, Germany, Italy and France have always given to composers resident on their soil an inalienable orientation. This unconscious Americanism is not always easy to see from here; from abroad it is visible to practically any one's naked eye.

That the gigantic flowering of musical composition that is already so far advanced here could be hindered by the Philharmonic's continuing to hide its head in the sand is absurd. We have come to fruition without its aid; we can go our way without its climbing on our bandwagon. I am not certain that it can get on without us, however. The W. P. A. has changed all that, the W.P.A. and the radio. Thirty thousand symphony orchestras in the United States, most of them founded since 1930, are playing American music today; and millions are listening to it with pleasure. It is a relief from stale standard repertory. Composers' Forum-Laboratories in a dozen cities have sharpened the musical public's discrimination, have pierced through the composer's frustration and solitude, have shown everybody that good will toward the authorship of musical works can produce a more lively musical occasion than all the Little Caesarism in the world exercised upon the defenseless dead. If the American music lover should continue in the next few years progressively to turn his attention away from the rendition of music and to study more its design, as he does seem inclined to do, the Philharmonic will have to move over our way; or else it will be out of the picture. I understand its Crossley rating on the air fell off last year from ten million to eight and a half, and a radio executive has told me that the listening public for any orchestral program seems to care more about what is played than about who conducts. Toscanini's conducting, for instance, which can be so electrifying in a hall, is, comparatively speaking, a flop in the American home. Barbirolli gets by, so far as he does, by the fact that 3 o'clock, Eastern Standard, of a Sunday afternoon is a nationally convenient hour to listen to serious music and also by the fact that the Philharmonic, for all its jitteriness, is a better orchestra, man by man, than the N. B. C., the only other symphonic group enjoying regularly a national hook-up.

And so, if the Philharmonic wishes to keep its place in American musical life, I think it needs to face squarely the fact that America, under its very nose, is changing from a music consumer into a music producer and to put its policy in line with the change. I think, therefore, that it should ease off on repeating Brahms and Beethoven and start playing the music of our century. It should play not only Americans and American residents but all the modern European music out of which these were born. And it should choose out of the vast repertory of the Romantic, the Rococo and the Baroque masters (a repertory barely skimmed now) all the works that explain or that set off by contrast the works of the modern masters and of us their progeny, the only possible legitimate center of emphasis in a vigorous musical culture.

V.T.: Article of May 26, 1941

Fa Sol La Fa Sol La Mi Fa

NASHVILLE, Tenn., May 25.—These are the syllables used by oldsters in rural regions of the South to intone the major scale, exactly as they were used in the British Isles long before Shakespeare. Indeed, the Elizabethan Fa La La is no more than a conventional reference to the habit of singing any part song first with the tonal syllables, so that melodies may be learned before words are attempted. So, still is the custom in all those parts of America where "The Sacred Harp" and "Southern Harmony" are used as singing books.

The former is common in Georgia, the Carolinas, Kentucky, Tennessee, Alabama, Arkansas, Louisiana and Texas. It has been reissued four times since its first appearance in 1844 and has sold upward of five million copies.

The "Southern Harmony," published in 1835, sold a half million copies before the Civil War, then was out of print till the Federal Writers' Project of Kentucky, under the sponsorship of the Young Men's Progress Club of Benton, Marshall County, reprinted it in facsimile in 1939.

By far the most celebrated in musicology circles of all the American song books, since Dr. George Pullen Jackson, of Vanderbilt University, revealed it to the learned world in "White Spirituals in the Southern Uplands," its usage among the folk is confined today to a very small region in southwest Kentucky. William ("Singing Billy") Walker, its author, considered it so highly that he ever after signed himself, even on his tombstone, A. S. H., meaning author of "Harmony." Today it is used by about forty old people, who meet every year at the County Court House of Benton and sing from 9 till 4. I went to hear the Southern harmony singing this year, lest it cease to exist before another, though most of the ancients looked healthy enough, I must say, and sang with a husky buzz; and a handful of youngsters of forty or more seemed active in perpetuating the style and repertory of it all.

The style is that of all back-country vocalism: a rather nasal intonation, a strict observance of rhythm and note (plus certain traditional ornaments and off tones) and no shadings of an expressive nature at all. Each song is sung first with the Fa Sol La syllables and then with its words. Various persons take turns at leading. The effect of the syllable singing is rather that of a Mozart quintet for five oboes. The effect of the verbal singing rather that of a fourteenth or fifteenth century motet.

The repertory is all the grand and ancient melodies that our Protestant ancestors brought to America in the seventeenth and eighteenth centuries. Most are pentatonic and hexatonic, many of them Dorian or Phrygian in mode. The part writing is French fifteenth century. There are usually three parts, a bass, a tenor (the melody) and a treble. Both of the latter are doubled at the octave by women and men, making of the whole a five-part piece. Since chords of the open fifth are the rule and parallel fifths common, the addition of these constant octaves gives to the whole an effect at once of the greatest antiquity and of the most rigorous modernity. Each part is a free melody, constantly crossing above or below the others; no mere harmonic filling attenuates the rigid contrapuntal democracy. There is something of the bagpipe, too, in the sound of it all, as well as in the configuration of many of the tunes.

Though the words are always sacred words (often of high poetic quality), neither the "Southern Harmony" nor "Sacred Harp" singings are, strictly speaking, religious manifestations. The proof of that is the fact that they have never become involved in the sectarian disputes that are the life of religion. Religion is rather the protective dignity under which a purely musical rite is celebrated. That rite is the repetition year after year of a repertory that is older than America itself, that is the musical basis of almost everything we make, of Negro spirituals, of cowboy songs, of popular ballads, of blues, of hymns, of doggerel ditties, of all our operas and symphonies.

It contains our basic conceptions of melody, of rhythm and of poetic prosody. It contains in addition the conception of freedom in part-uniting that has made of our jazz and swing the richest popular instrumental music in the world.

To persons traveling southward I do not recommend the "Southern Harmony" singing as the best introduction to the richness of style and repertory. The ancients are too few in number and too note-bound, and the singing is far too slow for nervous city taste. Easier to find on any summer Sunday and more lively in tone and rhythm are the devotees of the "Sacred Harp." The style and repertory are similar, but the vigor of the rendition is greater. If possible, buy a book and learn to sing yourself from the square and triangular notes. It is more fun that way.

G.P.: Memo of May 27, 1941

Dear Virgil:

The Sunday piece on the Philharmonic and the Monday piece on the Fa Sol La Singers seemed to me tops for the year. In addition to the excellent wisdom and entertaining writing that they contain, they had a quality of steadiness that struck me as the final touch of perfection in your style. Anybody reading either piece without having read you before or knowing anything about you, would instinctively feel, "Here is a man who knows what he is writing about, who is uninfluenced by irrelevancies of personality and whose judgment I can completely trust. I may disagree with that judgment and with his point of view, but I can't live without it."

Congratulations!

G.P.
[signed] Geoffrey

VI

G.P.: Memo of November 11, 1941

Dear Virgil:

I was wrong about your sentence that included "crematorium,"[10] and you were right. I checked up the next morning, and it was in the same sentence that you spoke of light opera, and in effect restricted your slap to that field.

10. The passage Parsons refers to occurs in a review of November 6, 1941, of Offenbach's *La Vie Parisienne* as presented by the New Opera Company at the 44th Street Theater. The offending passage reads: "As a musical show 'La Vie Parisiénne' makes the rest of Broadway both look and sound silly; and this applies to the Thirty-ninth Street crematorium [i.e., the Metropolitan Opera House] as well, whenever that ancient and honorable institution tries to do light opera."

But---.

I think the episode is rather revealing evidence of what can't be done in a newspaper critique. As I once told you, people who write for newspapers generally develop certain instinctive principles by which they work. They often have difficulty in giving reasons for what they do, but their practices are usually founded on long and sad truth. The essential point is, I think, that newspapers are not read carefully by most of their readers. You can rely upon a few intensely interested or learned persons who read your criticisms as carefully as they would read a book or a magazine article in a serious one like "Modern Music." But the average reader, even the intelligent one, in this speedway that we call a city, has to do his reading at the breakfast table, in the subway, or in snatches wherever he can find the time.

You gain enormously in public by writing in a newspaper, but you also lose something. I am convinced that certain kinds of subtlety have no place in the newspaper, precisely because of this item of hasty reading. I know that some years ago we all decided on the Editorial Page that satirical writing must be used with the greatest of care and the satire writ large if used at all. The point was that what seemed to us very neat satire was misunderstood by a whole parcel of readers who sat down to write us indignant letters.

I admit I read your review hastily. But most of your readers did likewise, and you have to write for this larger public whether you want to or not. That is the price you pay for the extraordinary power and influence that a critic on a great daily paper wields.

Mrs. Reid's[11] point was a little different, but I think

11. Helen Reid, wife of the owner of the *Herald-Tribune,* Odgen Reid. In his memoirs Thomson says of Mrs. Reid, ". . .though we shared mutual admiration, I almost invariably rubbed her the wrong way. My impishness and my arrogance were equally distasteful and something in my own resistance to her dislike of being rubbed the wrong way led me over and over again to the verge of offense." Thomson, *Virgil Thomson,* p. 331.

amounted to the same idea. She was really shocked and horrified by your statement that it was necessary to overstate a point at times in order to make your point. I think the question of hasty reading is the justification for her reaction. Such exaggeration as you had in mind is perfectly legitimate if you have the complete attention of your audience. It is utterly misleading, dangerous for the paper, and most unfair to your own reputation in the jumbled casual reading to which the columns of a newspaper are subjected.

I guess my principles for critical work on a large daily boil down to two:

The first we have been over and I am sure you understand. In fact, you understood it before you went to work, although the application of it required learning. That is the search for and use of the right word. Inevitably this search eliminates slang except in the very rare cases where the slang word is the right word. When you use a word like "wow," you confuse your reader as much as you enlighten him, — et cetera, et cetera.

The second point is the one I tried to write about today as a result of our talk the other evening of Mrs. Reid's reaction. It clips your wings as a writer somewhat, but I am sure it is an inescapable rule if you would go far as a critic on the Herald Tribune. I think I summed it up the other evening on the corner of 40th Street and 7th Avenue by saying that in every judgment you formed and uttered you must be on your knees to the exact truth of the event described.

G.P.
[signed] Geoffrey

VII

V.T.: Review of November 19, 1942
Grosso Modo
CONCERT by the Philharmonic-Symphony Orchestra in

Carnegie Hall last night under the direction of Arthur Rodzinski. The program follows:

Symphony No. 2 in D major	Beethoven
Spirituals in Five Movements	Gould
Symphony No. 5	Shostakovitch

Arthur Rodzinski, who led the Philharmonic last night, is a more interesting conductor to watch than to listen to. It is obvious that the mechanics of every score he plays are recorded in his brain and that he has an over-all, beginning-to-end memory of each piece's musical substance. He rehearses expeditiously and as thoroughly as time permits; when no audience is present he is very much the bigtime musical foreman. It is only in public that his indifference to the musical amenities shows up unfavorably.

Last night Beethoven's lovely Second Symphony came out violent, mechanical, fast and inaccurate. The strings messed up all the rapid figures and the short notes. The horns gurgled as if they were playing under water. The oboes buzzed and bleated. The heavy accents sounded as if some one had suddenly pinched the whole violin section. The music was clear in its essential outlines but soiled and unlovely, as in a good edition that has been carelessly handled.

Morton Gould's "Spirituals" didn't come off much better, and neither did the Shostakovitch Fifth Symphony. The horns continued to misbehave and Mr. Piastro's brief violin solo was out of tune. The orchestra sounded like a once-good machine wearing out. The conductor gave the effect of a competent engineer who was seeing to it that the machine didn't break down on the road but who couldn't be bothered coping with the absence of precision.

Not that there is much precision to cope with in the Gould score. It is a symphonic evocation of a cinematographic production number about musical comedy Negro life. It is diluted and unreal in spirit, heavily and coarsely glamorized in orchestration. The Shostakovitch Fifth is no masterwork, but it is a continuous and respectable piece of music. Its thin contrapuntal texture is not at all uninteresting to follow, and its themes are quite good. Unfortunately, it needs a blending of instrumental sounds, a care for balance and ensemble not unlike what chamber music requires, to keep the rather noble bareness of it from sounding hollow. Such blending, however, appeared to be no part of either the conductor's or the musicians' efforts. As a result, though the work held together rhythmically, its instrumental texture kept falling apart.

The Philharmonic program notes have apparently reached some kind of new low in literary style. There are howlers this week in every paragraph. I submit the following for the mixed metaphor prize:

"For a young man of thirty-six, Shostakovitch has known his fluctuations of status. Drama has hugged his career almost from the beginning. What's more, and if one were of a mind to explore the peaks and valleys of his achievements, there would undoubtedly be found more theater in the circumstances merely surrounding his composing than could be packed in a whole dynasty of Berliozes."

V.T.: Review of November 25, 1942

Itemized Account

"THE QUEEN OF SPADES," opera in three acts by Peter Ilyitch Tchaikovsky, after Pushkin, English version by Sumner Austin, presented last night at the Broadway Theater by the New Opera Company. . . .

Much of "The Queen of Spades" music is beautiful, and parts of it are expressive. Last night's rendition by the New Opera Company didn't bring out the best that is in the score by any means. It was, in fact, the least acceptable performance that this reviewer has heard yet out of the company's repertory.

I cannot recount here the complicated and somber story. I could not make out last night much of the English in which it was sung, though I sat in the sixth row. What I could get was in translationese that espoused neither the sentiments nor the melodic line correctly. The scenery was partly leftovers from last year's "Cosi Fan Tutte" and the costumes appeared to have been hired. The ballet was without style, the stage direction sketchy and the cast utterly unconvincing dramatically. Musically it was pretty amateurish, too, though there were bits of agreeable singing.

Miss Winifred Heidt, who played the aged countess, sang handsomely. Miss Mary Henderson, the heroine, has a pretty voice when she doesn't force. She lacks diction, style and stage presence, however; and her acting is non-existent. Mr. Hugh Thompson, the prince, sang his love song nicely, though it lay a little high for him. Mr. Norbert Ardelli, the tenor lead, would have been more nearly acceptable in a suburban performance of "Pagliacci." Miss Christine Johnson has an alto voice of lovely quality and good training. The chorus was both vigorous and pleasant, the orchestra neither.

If the reader can gather from these assorted comments an idea of what the musical performance was like as a whole, he will be doing better than I could do in the theater. Because it wasn't like anything as a whole. Good and bad moments succeeded one another without any predictability. The show seemed to have been thrown together haphazardly. It had neither continuity nor style and showed little evidence of responsible supervision. It is too bad, because the opera has dramatic power and musical interest. But it is not one that gets itself gracefully onto a stage without a certain amount of care. I was left with no general impression at all when I came away, only a memory of many ineptitudes.

G.P.: Memo of November 25, 1942

I regret to disturb your Thanksgiving Day peace of mind but in justice to the paper as well as yourself, I feel I must tell you how badly I think you slipped in the last week or so.

I suspect that if I had been Managing Editor I would have fired you out of hand for putting that word "beaut" in that otherwise excellent review of the Boston concert.[12] At the least

12. Thomson's review of November 25, 1942, of the Boston Symphony contains the statement "The Martinu Symphony is a beaut."

I would have notified you that if ever again a word of slang appeared in any of your reviews, you need not report for work the next day. I assure you that all your strongest admirers feel about such a sour note exactly as I do. As for the casual readers, I am sure it completely upsets any confidence they may have formed in your judgment. Just as a detail, even your use of slang was wrong. "Beaut" has taken on in the last few years an unfavorable connotation. If one had a shiner, one would say it was a "beaut," for example. But that is a detail. The real point is that such jarring notes belittle you in the eyes of nine out of ten readers — 99 out of 100, I should guess.

Then came your review of the Tchaikovsky opera this morning. It seems to me a perfect example of how not to write a musical review. You showed no perspective about the fact that it was a new company, or a first performance, and your only analysis of the whole effect was based on a number of unrelated items. Fundamentally it is a lack of perspective that you show in all these blunders. It is not that you should praise what you disapprove, or alter your standards in any way. It is simply that you fail to convey to the reader the background of the performance and your own consciousness of that background. Incidentally, if I see the word "amateurish" in your column again, I shall scream. I haven't the faintest idea of what you mean by the word, and I don't believe you have. If a performance lacks style or distinction, or is stilted or stiff, or what not, say so. To my ear the use of "amateurish" is a lazy generalization for lack of the more accurate word. But that is again a detail. The main point is that you don't view the occasion as a whole in relation to the musical life of the city, the potential growth of the undertaking, et cetera.

In a lesser degree the same considerations apply to your last Philharmonic review. I feel sure that your criticisms were accurate in detail. But surely there is a broader approach to the problem of the Philharmonic. If a horn sounded as if it were blowing under water and you felt you should say so, I think you should also add the fact that he was one of the finest horn blowers in the country. The strings too can play like angels at times. What I am getting at is that by a broader approach in your criticism of something like the Philharmonic, attacking the really vulnerable features of the organization, you would accomplish far more than you do by such pro- fessorial, examination-paper-marking criticism as you gave. The detail is important, but the general effect and the reasons for the general effect are the vital points. This particular review was excellently written and an entertaining piece of work, but I am sure it failed to carry conviction to most of those who heard the concert, for the very lack of the human touch that I have referred to above. Anyone who sits in judgment as you do, should be damned modest and generous, remembering the personal equations involved, the difficulties of an orchestra which faces a period of short funds, etc., etc.

I hoped I would never have to say it again, but I must. Last spring you were at the bottom of the valley—the bottom of the brook, if you prefer. You had gradually crawled out until you were, say, one-third of the way up the slope. In these last weeks I feel you have slipped clear to the bottom again. The thing that readers most want from a critic is a reliance on his judgment. When you use slang, or become petty and personal in your criticisms, you compromise yourself with all your readers. For Christ sake, what is the matter with you?

[signed] Geoffrey

P.S. I think, your smarty head[line] on the opening of the opera was another item that showed a complete lack of perspective.[13] It was neither clever nor appropriate. After all, here is a famous institution carrying on in war time against

13. Thomson's review of November 24, 1942, of Donizetti's *Daughter of the Regiment* as presented by the Metropolitan Opera, contains the headline "Monkey Business as Usual."

tremendous obstacles. Every one of your readers knows that such is the situation and when you failed to pay any attention to these factors in your review, you irritated and shocked them.

VIII

V.T.: Review of December 4, 1943

A Slow Show

"RIGOLETTO," opera in three acts by Giuseppe Verdi, book by Piave, adapted from Victor Hugo's play "Le Roi s'amuse": first performance of the season at the Metropolitan Opera last night. . . .

"Rigoletto," as given last night at the Metropolitan Opera House, was labored and slow, excepting for the very dramatic last act, which sounded out quite handsomely and moved with vigor. Lily Pons, the official star of the evening, sang prettily enough in her pale and bird-like fashion. Jan Peerce, who, without ever having crossed the Atlantic, has become our best Italian tenor, did a piece of work that was both robust and distinguished. Mr. [Lawrence] Tibbett did not do well in the title part, and the pacing of the opera as a whole was funereal.

"Rigoletto" is not an opera that ever gets going before the third act. The first two have some good numbers in them, like the famous "Caro Nome" aria, but they lack excitement and continuity. This fault was exaggerated last night by Mr. [Cesare] Sodero's lax conducting. He gave the singers their head, as if they were old-style virtuosos. Being nothing of the sort, they all dragged and mostly flatted (excepting Mr. Peerce) whenever they got the bit in their teeth. And a work already discontinuous went soggy and slow, just as it always does in Italy when the conductor fails to use the whip.

The third act, which is usually easier to bring off with unity, was no livelier than its predecessors. But the fourth, which goes of itself, was animated and interesting. Mr. Peerce's "La donna e mobile" and the quartet were handsomely rendered. Anna Kaskas, who sang Maddalena, and Nicola Moscona, the Sparafucile, were excellent. The orchestral storm was fine fun, and the whole show sailed before a fair wind till it hit doldrums again in Miss Pons's and Mr. Tibbett's final duet.

I am afraid that it was Mr. Tibbett's lamentable vocal insufficiency in a role that is long, difficult and responsible which sank the show as surely as Mr. Sodero's complaisant accompaniments did. Miss Pons worked seriously and carefully, but her voice is too small to take the lead in operatic ensemble-singing. She is at her best in arpeggiated solo crooning. That she did neatly and right on pitch. But she is not much of an actress, either. She has a certain presence and she is a good musician. I suppose it is fire she lacks, the warmth of the real theatrical temperament. And I do wish that somebody would slap her hands every time she arranges her train or pulls her skirt away from her girdle. That sort of thing betrays a preoccupation with personal appearance that is as fatal to musical concentration as it is to dramatic illusion.

V.T.: Review of December 6, 1943

Two Thomases, Two Debuts

"MIGNON," opera in three acts, music by Ambroise Thomas, book by Barbier and Carre, revival at the Metropolitan Opera House Saturday night. . . .

The revival of "Mignon" last Saturday night at the Metropolitan Opera House did honor to the work's composer, Ambroise Thomas, and to its conductor, Sir Thomas Beecham. Sir Thomas's orchestral rendering and general pacing of this lovely music were delicate, vigorous, grand. The rest of the proceedings, what took place on the stage, visually and vocally, was aptly summed up by one of my colleagues of the press as "amateur night."

Nobody, literally nobody in the cast, sang consistently in any way that musicians consider legitimate. Miss [Risë] Stevens and Mr. [Norman] Cordon were the most professional sounding. But the former forced and misplaced her beautiful voice in a most irregular fashion and mugged around the stage for all the world as if the audience were a cameraman come to photograph her teeth, while the latter sang with constricted throat and stalked about stiffly. Miss [Lucielle] Browning and Mr. [John] Gurney, being artists of lesser natural resources, were less disappointing, though nothing either did had much style. Mr. [James] Melton's vocalism, as always, was naif and his dramatic performance vague. He does have, however, a certain forthrightness in his work that is not without charm; and there is a blitheness about him that holds attention. Both these qualities give to his performances a minimum of adequacy; real distinction waits upon the improvement of his vocal technique.

Of the evening's two debutants Mr. Donald Dame was the more satisfactory all 'round. In fact, his was the most nearly distinguished performance of any in the cast. He sang nicely for the most part and acted convincingly. Without being at present a singer or actor of any extraordinary mastery, he impressed me as being a dependable artist and one likely to be very useful in the company.

Miss Patrice Munsel, though a young woman of phenomenal talents, is far from being prepared for present glory. She has an unschooled voice of wide range and considerable power. In one or two passages it was clear that if she learns how to use it properly before she uses it up she may well have a great singing career later. Whether it remains a high coloratura or develops downward, as many such youthful voices do with maturing womanhood, is unpredictable.

If she continues to abuse it in public as she did last night, it may well in short time turn into a cracked whisper. Miss Munsel has a remarkable voice, a good ear and musical intelligence. Her natural gifts are so great that it would be unfortunate indeed if she embarked on a career of public appearance before training had disciplined these gifts and strengthened them to stand the wear and tear of professional exploitation.

Miss Munsel seems to be a born trouper, nevertheless. She has confidence, aplomb, personal radiation. Her stage quality, though definitely on the flashy side, is permeated by real temperament. Her dramatic characterization the other evening and her physical movements were as incisive as the timbre of her voice. If her whole performance, vocal and dramatic, is sustained at present more by the sheer sang-froid of childhood than by training, that does not mean that the former could not be replaced in a few years' time by the latter. It is sincerely to be hoped that Miss Munsel, having now shown the public her high possibilities, will put childish things, like dreams of an immediately glorious career, behind her and settle down to learn some dependable form while waiting for her vocal organ to mature. The idea that any female voice of seventeen is ripe for big time is the sheerest folly to entertain.

G.P.: Memo of December 8, 1943

Dear Virgil:

No doubt you will have reached the same conclusion for yourself by this time, but just to check from my own reaction, — the two detailed reviews of performances at the Metropolitan went pretty sour. We have had a pretty rapid sprinkling of angry protests from operagoers. I don't lay much stress upon them except as they support my own reaction.

Both reviews, it seemed to me, fell into the error which it took so long to cure Bohm[14] of when he first came to the paper—that of marking an examination paper. The chief objection to such a review is its dullness. Only people who were actually present in the opera house have the remotest interest in such a detailed writing. In addition, the general effect is bad, I am sure, since it assumes a degree of wisdom and capacity to judge offhand which, as we have often discussed, irritates profoundly the average cultivated reader. There must be a realization of the obstacles and a generous approach on

14. Jerome D. Bohm, a staff music critic for the *Tribune*.

the part of a critic if he is to make any headway with his audience.

I am sorry that you got off on the wrong foot in these two criticisms for I feel you can do a swell job of constructive criticism with respect to the Met. You will defeat your own ends and destroy your influence if you sound like a carping school teacher rapping his pupils over their knuckles. There is one point which I think you have simply got to take cognizance of—and not just take cognizance of, but reveal to the reader that you are aware of the fact that we are at war and that any sort of artistic production is gravely handicapped at the outset, —another reason for leaning over back to be generous. As a corrective to these two missteps, why not avoid criticising anybody by name for a while? Criticise the production, criticise the orchestra, etc. Otherwise single out for specific mention only the people you can praise. Come to think of it, that's not such a bad general rule anyway. I couldn't help but feel that your delightful piece on Beebe and the opera[15] would have been stronger if you had left out the names of the three glamorous soloists. I think your inclusion of Marian Anderson, for instance, simply misled your readers. There is certainly nothing glamorous about her. She is a special case with a special appeal outside of her musical value, but obviously you didn't have time to go into all of that. I am sure the piece would have been stronger if you had simply described the general type and let the idea sink in.

Respectfully submitted,
G.P.
[signed] Geoffrey

---

15. Lucius Beebe, a *Tribune* columnist, had complained about the emphasis on glamor at the Metropolitan Opera at the expense of musical quality. Thomson's Sunday column of November 28, 1943, expanded on this idea.

Restructuring Education: The Contemporary Music Project

Contrary to the classroom experience of most teachers, a generation has grown up in the United States for whom music is at the center of life. "Indeed," reports Charles Reich, "the new music has achieved a degree of integration of art into everyday life that is probably unique in modern societies; to find anything comparable one would have to look to the Middle Ages or primitive men. Like a medieval cathedral or the carvings in a tribal village, the art of rock is constantly present as a part of everyday life, not something to be admired in a museum or listened to over coffee after dinner and the day's work are done. It is significant that nearly everyone who deeply feels the music also makes an attempt at playing an instrument and even at composing. For the lover of rock, as for men in earlier times, art is a daily companion to share, interpret and transfigure every experience and emotion."[1]

1. Charles A. Reich, *The Greening of America,* paperback ed. (New York: Bantam Books, 1971), p. 262.

Martha Hayes, former choral director for a high school in Dallas, has had frustrating experience of what Reich describes. During the mid-1960s her singers were forming instrumental and vocal groups outside class and composing for them. She wanted to draw on this vitality and develop it, but she was "boxed in" by the school's requirement that she prepare standardized concert programs. The vitality of culture among "untrained" young people was brought home to another high school teacher, Thayne Tolle, when he was teaching a musicianship course in Wichita. It was not the band and orchestra players who were most inventive, but the rock musicians. Compositions by the latter included nonmetric works for such sound sources as electric guitar, electronic pulsators, and tuned bottles. Students with a school music background tended to copy Brahms or Saint-Saëns. Thom Mason remembers the feeling of isolation among his fellow music majors in college because they could not improvise and play popular music the way other students could.

Experiences such as these helped to establish the fostering of creativity as CMP's central goal in curriculum reform. As Robert Washburn stated in outlining a comprehensive musicianship course for high schools in New York State, "Most important [the course] may stimulate the elements of creativity inherent in every human being and help the students to identify and begin to develop their own abilities in the field of music."[2]

CMP adherents agree that traditional methods of music education inhibit creativity. One of Merrill Bradshaw's experiences at Brigham Young University is typical. He once combined a comprehensive musicianship class of "average" students with a traditional theory class of "honors" students. Whereas the former were eager to experiment with the new

2. Robert Washburn et al. *Comprehensive Foundations of Music: A One-Year Elective Course for High School Students* (Albany, N.Y.: N.Y. State Dept. of Education, 1971), p. 25.

ideas he suggested, the honors people hesitated. "How do you want me to do it?" they asked. "How much will it count toward my grade?"

The explanation for these attitudes seems to lie in the factorylike model of traditional music schools. Immediately upon entry, both faculty and students are classified as "applied," "theory," "musicology," "ethnomusicology," "music education," and the like. Each subdivision of the faculty sets up skill specifications against which its students are measured. Over the years, as specifications become refined, the training gets narrower. "Theory" becomes "harmony," which becomes "chords," and in extreme cases real music is discarded from the theory classroom because chord-labeling skills develop more rapidly if synthetic chord progressions are substituted. The same reductionism occurs in musicology, where students often sacrifice original research to study past Ph.D. exams, and in music education, where students often sacrifice sight-reading skills because they have to learn to play the National Anthem.

Such education produces students who cannot relate counterpoint in one class with harmony in another, who know the terms for forms but not the processes that create them, who get A's in harmony class and fail their senior exams, who get bored and drop out of school music groups. Other results can be seen in the teachers. They also had certain of their abilities selected for development, and now they process these skills in others. According to William Thomson of the University of Arizona, "Many of them have stopped listening and responding to music." Karl Korte of the University of Texas says that they are "tied to what they were taught 25 years ago." Leaders at CMP's teacher workshops often had difficulty getting such people to talk about music. Vernon Kliewer of Indiana University thinks they were afraid to make mistakes or express doubts —to say, "I'm not sure but I think I heard this" or "This may not work but let's try it and see what happens."

The CMP leaders I spoke to all agreed that students will not be creative if their teachers are rigid. They said that in their own work they always seek learning experiences for themselves, for example, using some music each year that is unfamiliar to them, or encouraging student projects in areas they have not studied themselves. "I never use the same course outline twice," they said. "I change the pieces every term so I won't grow stale." They often apologized for not being able to remember the sequence of events during the semester just past. "It always changes." "I don't know what happened next. It always depends on what happened in class. I couldn't teach without letting it happen as the students get to it."

Robert Gauldin of the Eastman School of Music feels that the best teaching is not necessarily done by those who are the most proficient technically. It is done by people who are open to new ideas, who are willing to question things, who have an outgoing quality that infects others with a desire to expand and to change. Supporting this is Karl Korte's observation that high school teachers were often the most flexible participants at CMP workshops. "They lead a less cloistered life. They're being continually challenged. College teachers are apt to deal only with music majors."

Martha Hayes in Dallas reports that she was both troubled and excited by the new possibilities she saw as a student of CMP's Martin Mailman. She had to face a lot of things she didn't know. Her chief worry was, "Do I have the potential?" Her advice to others is to keep trying. "Those who find they don't have the full potential within themselves will find other resources to supplement their teaching."

"Naturally everybody prefers the most knowledgeable and the most able person," says Eunice Boardman, formerly of Wichita State. "But that's not necessary. It's your willingness to plunge in with students and learn that makes the difference. It's the freedom to admit, I've never had a chance to do this and you'll probably do it better than I will. What we're doing is questioning the old European idea that teachers are authorities."

In changing their studio and classroom methods, the teachers I talked to emphasized two specific goals: 1) to help their students take "a fresh look" at music, and 2) to help them understand the elements that are common to all musics, not just those emphasized in Western art music.

Several CMP teachers have used group improvisations for these purposes, most often with nonstandard sound sources such as dwarf instruments. Mary Ann Saulman starts her high school students in Chapman, Kan. on an exploration of sound with two simple and disarmingly avant-garde assignments:

> Experiment No. 1: Try to find silence within a 15-minute period of time. Make a list of any sounds which intrude upon the silence you are seeking.

> Experiment No. 2: Make a list of interesting sounds around your home or neighborhood. Be ready to describe these sounds in terms of their elements: pitch, duration, timbre, intensity.

Robert Trotter of the University of Oregon has found that Asian and African musics are ideal for initiating a fresh inquiry into the nature of music. He says that students like the excitement of exploring unknown territory where new concepts of rhythm and timbre may arouse new curiosities and touch new feelings. Violent juxtapositions among recorded classroom examples is a favorite waking-up device of Robert Gauldin. He finds that this technique works even when all the music is from the Western concert tradition. For maximum impact, however, Trotter feels that the Western concert tradition must be de-emphasized. He recommends that five musical repertories be given equal time: 1) Western concert music to 1950, 2) Western concert music since 1950, 3) contemporary popular music, 4) European and American folk music, 5) African and Asian musics.

The "common elements" approach, which CMP advocated, centers on the processes of music and typically involves creative input from students. For example, after studying Varèse's *Density 21.5* for solo flute, Leo Kraft of Queens College in New York asked his students to compose solo pieces to be performed and discussed in class. The purpose of the assignment was to show how register can be used to shape a musical work. Also at Queens, Thom Mason used a similar activity in conjunction with the Ives *Unanswered Question*. His class planned a group improvisation that would embody the gesture of the Ives but incorporate different sound material. Earlier in the year Mason had asked for one-minute pieces for two pitch classes. This restriction in pitch automatically forced people to shape their compositions by means of durations, ranges, articulations, and dynamics—some of the fundamental resources that students tend to overlook in listening and analysis assignments.

When Martha Hayes asked her high school students to supply additional examples of the musical resources she had introduced, Gospel records were brought in to illustrate vocal techniques, Ravi Shankar records to illustrate time systems, and a Dave Brubeck album to illustrate polymeter and improvisation. To illustrate the concept of canonic variation, one of Saulman's students brought two ping-pong balls to class, which he dropped on the floor one after the other. The need for open spaces in music was brought home to John McManus's high school band in McMinneville, Ore., when a player composed a work in which pitches and durations were based on throws of dice. The process produced an unpleasantly thick and noisy work, and immediately the idea occurred to several players that some throws of the dice should be used for rests.

In developing an awareness of processes and general principles, questions apparently are more effective than statements. Martha Hayes says that high school students are fully prepared to discuss such topics as, What creates the musical interest in this piece? or What creates its shape? Norman Hessert of Moorhead State College in Minnesota spends more than half his class time on student compositions and on questions such as, Did you like it? Why? What was the shape? Did it work for you? Did the composer succeed in what he set out to do? How could he do better? Is the notation clear? Is it appropriate for the piece? Was the performance satisfactory? If there were problems, did they exist in the music or in the way it was played?

Eunice Boardman used to ask her pedagogy classes, What is it you want to teach? What music will do this? What will help a child to understand the composer's intention? How can you use a song to help children grow? Instead of teaching specific children's pieces, which is the usual approach to pedagogy, she would ask her students to find things on their own that illustrate specific musical processes, then to explain their choices to the class, then, finally, to teach each other these songs.

Everyone at CMP was skeptical of exams and grades as an accurate measure of student abilities and achievement. In training Texas college teachers to handle comprehensive musicianship courses, Martin Mailman found that "more often than not, problems that occurred in presenting information or developing skills proved to be 'hang-ups' within the instructors rather than deficiencies in the students."[3] According to Robert Trotter, placement tests "are very primitive in evaluating promise in a student. We give students too narrow a view of

3. Martin Mailman et al., *Comprehensive Musicianship in the Junior College* (Washington, D.C.: CMP, 1971), p. 6.

what they can become." Merrill Bradshaw agrees. He once taught fundamental music skills to a group of "failures" at Brigham Young University. "They had good ears," he says. "It was just that the system was getting between them and sound." He used group improvisations to get the students to make musical decisions based on what they heard. This gave them the confidence to work on more traditional skills, with the result that all but one of them was able to meet departmental requirements.

Bradshaw dislikes exams because "they force you to teach things you can justify with a grade. That means always being safe in what you do in class." As one alternative he and his colleagues at Brigham Young have developed a computerized musicianship profile to provide a continuing evaluation of the musical competencies of each student. It is not a grading device but a tool used in recommending courses and/or remedial work. Thayne Tolle says that he "can't grade creatively." When he was teaching high school students he never put grades on papers. Instead he commented on the substance of each person's work. His only tests were over fundamentals, and they were mainly to see if he or his students had missed anything. Most of the composition experiences John McManus developed for use in his high school band would have floundered if he had graded the pieces his players wrote. Grades would have made everybody afraid to fail. There would have been no spirit of adventure. As it turned out, "mistakes" rather than "successes" provided the major openings for discussions of how musical processes work. Billie Erlings, a class-piano teacher, says that she dislikes keyboard exams because they tend to substitute a series of technical hurdles for what she wants the piano to become for her students — an aid in their continuing musical growth.

As an alternative to formal exams, Vernon Kliewer of Indiana University uses individual projects and private conferences. In 1971 Trotter gave one of his classes a written explanation why he was dispensing with grades altogether and adopting a "pass-no pass" system. Among his reasons were:

> Because a large proportion of quantifiable intellectual competencies develop slowly, requiring much practice in a spirit of long-range personal involvement and in a spirit of self-confidence often threatened by judgmental tests.

> Because a class free of such tests provides the best opportunity for students to develop internal motivation related to the objectives of the course by freeing them from the external pressure to learn something merely in order to pass a test.

In his high school musicianship classes Thayne Tolle used to give two grades, *A* if all assignments were completed and *C* if some were not. One year, however, he had a student who came to all the classes, was attentive, but took no active part in the classwork. He merely wanted to absorb what was going on. Tolle had to fail him, and he still regrets it.

Another alternative to authoritarian testing and grading is self-evaluation. For example, Marguerite Miller, who teaches piano at Wichita State, asks her students to analyze their own technical deficiencies and compose remedial etudes. She wants to know what a student's self-image is: Is this student aware that he has a rhythmic problem? What does a student mean when he says he has "no technique"? Is the student with "no problem" listening to himself? Miller meets with her students as a group so that they can evaluate each other's progress. She says that guidance of this sort, together with constant questioning about how each new piece should be approached, has made her students "more independent. I feel confident that they can go out and deal with any new piece and come up with a valid performance."

In orchestration classes at the University of Texas, Karl

Korte often has students work from piano reductions of ensemble pieces so that they can compare their work with that of a master composer. Robert Gauldin encourages self teaching by dividing his theory classes at the Eastman School into small groups for discussions of analysis and composition assignments. He says that the students not only give competent advice to each other but also provide the individual attention he himself cannot give when classes are large. With improvisation assignments Thom Mason is concerned only with how close a student comes to achieving what he sets out to do. "I do not evaluate if I liked it. But if a group improv is supposed to be a group experience and it turns out to be a string of solos, then it hasn't worked." In regard to composition, everyone agreed that if the assignment is clearly formulated and if works are played and discussed in class, there is general agreement about how "successful" they have been.

Another major reform adopted by CMP adherents relates to the role of textbooks and to the sequence of learning experiences in the course of a semester. The attitude toward textbooks was unequivocal. "They don't work," said Merrill Bradshaw, "so why not throw them out?" In all types of class, from beginning theory to graduate school, the preferred alternative was to begin with pieces of music (performed live if possible) and to treat books as resources, assigning chapters here and there as needed. In this way a hundred or more compositions might be used in the course of a year. When I asked what books were consulted, I was often given a list of ten or twenty titles.

Part of the attitude toward texts is necessitated by the attitude toward class routine: Let the order of topics be determined by what happens in class. This principle guides the work of almost everyone I spoke to. They did not tackle a new topic because it was the next chapter in a book but because it was important at that moment to the people in the class. This procedure, they say, lends an atmosphere of urgency to the learning process, as when a high school student could not conduct the fermata in a band piece he had written and needed an on-the-spot lesson. Vernon Kliewer found a similar learning opportunity in one of his classes for nonmusic majors at Indiana. He had asked for one-minute pieces for any sound sources embodying the principle of varied repetition. One girl did a percussion piece for five players using objects from her dormitory room. Her intention was to repeat the durations and change the colors, but her analysis focused on rhythm, which she had not varied at all. Further discussion brought out that what she had done was to establish and vary a line of timbres. Thus was introduced a concept that many students find troublesome, *Klangfarbenmelodie*. In like manner Thom Mason does not "teach" forms. He finds that group improvisations and the discussions that follow eventually explicate all the standard forms, together with the processes that create them.

The problem of loose ends in this sort of teaching worries some people. The solution Billie Erlings uses is to assign student projects that will fill in the points missed in class. At Brigham Young three techniques have been used: 1) All students are given "I'd like to know" forms on which they write questions not covered in class. An appropriate faculty member then meets with each person individually. 2) A historical time chart has been installed in one classroom to clarify chronology. 3) Two hours a week (out of ten) are set aside for topics that the faculty feel might be neglected. In the past these sessions have included traditional counterpoint and part writing, the analysis of 12-tone music, and various periods of music history.

However, not everyone is worried about loose ends. Norman Hessert of Moorhead State College in Minnesota objects to the question. "Coverage is the wrong approach," he told me, "this idea that you have this much time and this much material to get through. My approach is to say that we have a certain amount of time. We'll be musicians together during this time, and when it is over we will all have expanded. In four years you are bound to cover everything." Robert Trotter said almost the same thing: "I don't feel pressure to 'get through' a body of material. We listen to as much music as we can and we talk together about these experiences. I don't think I'm supposed to provide everything. In fact my last word to every class is always 'and. . . .' "

Most of the reforms described to me were developed by individual instructors working alone in traditionally structured music departments. However, large-scale changes have also been instituted in some schools, among them Southern Methodist University in Dallas and the University of Oregon in Eugene. In both cases the changes took place when new administrators arrived—Robert Trotter at Oregon in 1963 and Gene Bonelli at SMU in 1969.

SMU, according to Bonelli, was ripe for change. Most of the faculty thought that the existing approach to theory was outdated. It was based almost entirely on Walter Piston's *Harmony*. It neglected twentieth-century repertory, creative experiences, and skills that could be applied in history, performance, and music education courses. Bonelli also concluded that departmental prerogatives and structures were inhibiting faculty growth. "It was too easy for new ideas to take a back seat to bureaucratic considerations." He wanted greater contact between faculties so that individuals could share their concerns for the overall training of students. Before his arrival, a violin instructor might have complained to other violinists that the theory department was not doing enough to develop rhythmic skills, but he would never have said so to the theory faculty. The latter, in turn, never had the chance to suggest remedies for use in the violinist's own studio.

Bonelli's first step was to create a one-year faculty committee to recommend revision. This was also Trotter's first step, and both administrators agree on the need for intensive faculty participation. "You cannot impose change on a faculty," Bonelli says. "It is absolutely necessary to have them involved and to have all objections voiced from the start."

Bonelli's committee recommended that a new department be formed, the Department of Musical Arts and Skills; that it consist of a cross-section of teachers from composition and theory, history and literature, music education, and performance; and that all students be enrolled in this department for their first two years, after which they could apply for admission to a specialized degree program. The new department administers four courses, which the students take concurrently: 1) "Materials, Structures, Skills," a four-hour-a-week course in compositional techniques, analysis, aural perception, music reading, and sight singing; 2) "Music Literature," a one-hour-a-week course drawing its repertory from the music used in (1), plus community and campus concerts; 3) private performance study plus a functional piano lab if necessary; 4) ensemble experience. Each of these courses is taught by a single instructor.

Trotter's committee also proposed a two-year core curriculum for entering students but preferred to have it administered by a committee rather than by a separate department. Two basic policies were established: 1) to give equal attention to each of Trotter's five musical repertories, and 2) to give equal attention to composition, performance, and analysis.

The core-curriculum concept has also been adopted by Moorhead State College, which now has a four-year musicianship course, each section of which meets seven hours a week.

At Brigham Young University all freshmen and sophomores attend a course called "Expanding Musicianship," which meets ten hours a week and includes theory, composition, literature, aural skills, and ensemble work. A typical project list for the first semester reads: 1) Write a piece for class performance using four pitches. 2) Perform a piece you are studying on your major instrument and analyze it for the class. 3) Choose some aspect of a historical style and involve the class in musical activities that will explicate the concept. 4) Devise a project of your own.

Both Trotter and Bonelli provided opportunities for their faculties to grow into this type of program. At Oregon team teaching was used in the comprehensive musicianship classes until each teacher felt confident about taking a section of his own. Now the staff meets together once a week to coordinate this classwork. Trotter encouraged all his staff members to expand their interests and to teach in more than one subject area. Bonelli asked his performance faculty to team-teach the implementation labs and also to perform and talk about the literature for their instruments in the comprehensive musicianship classes. Both administrators used their influence over appointments to get new people who had participated in CMP workshops.

Bonelli is convinced that change of this sort cannot succeed unless the chief administrator is committed to it. He has observed situations in which only one or two teachers pushed for change and failed, thereby making future attempts at innovation even more difficult. It would have been better, he feels, if the individual teachers had continued working within their own classes, expanding their repertories and techniques, incorporating creative experiences, loosening class routines, reinterpreting bureaucratic requirements, and seeking like-minded faculty in other departments for team-teaching projects.

Trotter agrees. He has seen departments fail to make meaningful changes because they "pussy-footed — they tried doing a little here and a little there. It doesn't work. We're talking about *fundamental* changes."

A newcomer to CMP, a pianist, asked me what I thought the CMP workshops were supposed to be doing. He had come "mostly to listen and get new teaching ideas," but he found that more than this was expected of him. He was supposed to talk, to analyze, to perform, to compose. "What are the goals here?" he asked. "Are we supposed to get students to like gamelan music instead of Beethoven? Should we see if we can merchandise Bach the way they do the Beatles?" A few weeks before, Thayne Tolle had observed, "I think a teacher should provide students with activities in music and aesthetics that will enable them to deal with music on their own terms and select for themselves what they need to enrich their own lives."

As Reich observes, "Our ideas of education are absurdly narrow and primitive for the kinds of tasks men face; education now is little more than training for the industrial army. What is needed is just the opposite of what we now have. A person should question what he is told and what he reads. He should demand the basis upon which experts or authorities have reached a conclusion. He should doubt his own teachers. He should believe that his own subjective feelings are of value. He should make connections and see relationships where the attempt has been made to keep them separate. He should appreciate the diversity of things and ideas rather than be told that one particular way is the 'right' way. He should be exposed and re-exposed to as wide a variety of experience and contrast as possible. Above all, he should learn to search for and develop his own potential, his own individuality, his own uniqueness. That is what the word 'educate' literally means. What we urgently need is not training but education, not indoctrination but the expansion of each individual—a process continuing throughout life."[4]

June-August 1972
(revised April 1975)

4. Reich, *The Greening*, p. 392.

Reassessing History: Music in The United States

In the sixteenth and seventeenth centuries, when Europeans began their conquest of the New World, the North American continent was the home of two or three million Americans, the Indians. Their greatest population densities were along the coasts and around the Great Lakes. To Europeans Indian culture appeared uniform across the land. In truth it encompassed a variety of language, dress, shelter, custom, ritual, and art that can hardly be imagined today. For example, between 1,000 and 2,000 languages were being spoken in North America in 1600.[1] At other times and places men have slaughtered more people than were killed during the conquest of North America, but never have men slaughtered so many cultures. By 1890, when the white man fought and won his last major battle with the Indians, only 250,000 of America's natives were alive, and all but 100 of America's native

This essay was published in Swedish in *Sohlmans Masiklexikon* 5 (Stockholm, 1976). Reprinted by permission.

1. Population and language statistics are from Harold E. Driver, *Indians of North America*, 2nd ed. (Chicago: University of Chicago, 1969).

languages had vanished. Nor did the arrogance of whites end there. Not until 1948 did Indians gain the right to vote in all states of their native land, and even today they are the poorest and shortest-lived people in the U.S.

It is impossible now to describe fully America's aboriginal music. Frederick Burton, an early student of Ojibway culture, observed that music for an Indian is not a separate category labeled *art*, nor is it performed in most cases by a professional class of musicians. It is part of everyone's daily life and, along with dance, an essential ingredient in ceremony and ritual.[2] More recently Bruno Nettl has identified six main stylistic regions: 1) Eskimo-Northwest coast, 2) the Great Basin (mostly Utah and Nevada), 3) California, 4) Athabascan (parts of Texas), 5) Plains-Pueblo area, and 6) the Eastern region. The most complex music, he writes, is found on the Northwest coast, around the Gulf of Mexico, and among the Pueblo Indians. The simplest music occurs in the Great Basin area. "The basic unit in Indian music is the song, which usually lasts (including a number of repetitions where this is customary) between 20 seconds and three minutes. The vast majority of the songs. . .include only a melody and have only one pitch sounding at a given moment. Purely instrumental music is rare. There is no solo drumming, and the only melodic instrumental music is that played on flutes and flageolets. . . .The combination of percussive accompaniment with vocal music is almost universal in North America."[3]

Burton was fascinated by the intervallic relationships in Ojibway music and by its melodic and rhythmic variability. He found "much vagueness in the Indian's frequent slurring from one tone to another, the intervals are often, to say the least, unexpected, their scale relationship hard to determine."

2. Frederick R. Burton *American Primitive Music* (New York, 1909; reissued Port Washington, N.Y.: Kennikat Press, 1969).

3. Bruno Nettl, *North American Indian Musical Styles,* American Folk-lore Society Memoires, vol. 45 (Philadelphia, 1954), p. 7.

He heard intervals of an eighth-tone and less. Repetitions of rhythmic and melodic ideas were never exact. He could find no systematic principle of variation and ornamentation. He once heard a singer accompany himself on a drum, combining 48 beats in the voice part with 35 on the drum. His conclusion was typically Western: Indian music is disorderly. It "rambles on" and "neglects necessary pauses." Indians, for their part, often found the white man's music monotonous. A German lieder recital, for example, sounded to an Indian friend of Burton's like the "same song over and over only that sometimes [the singer] made it long and sometimes short."[4]

Indian music has rarely been more than a curiosity to other Americans, and there has been no cross-fertilization among Indian and European cultures such as occurred between blacks and whites. In recent years some Indian handicrafts have come into vogue and a few recordings of tribal music have been released. But very soon in the conquest of North America the music and culture of America's natives were reduced to a few scattered and shriveled remains.

1600-1720

The earliest important European settlements in North America were established by Spain (beginning with St. Augustine, Fla., 1565) and later by England, France, and Holland. The only musical tradition from these early years that has been investigated in detail is that of the English settlers, whose descendents spearheaded the fight for independence from Europe and thereby set the future course of political, economic, and cultural life.

Instruments were difficult to transport across the ocean, and for the 18,000 Britishers who were in North America by

4. Burton, *American Primitive Music*, p. 95.

1640, music consisted mostly of singing. The repertory was more sacred than secular. The Puritan sect held that music could easily be abused as a purely worldly pleasure. Many Puritans, perhaps even a majority, believed that secular music was a waste of time and that singing the praises of God was the only worthy musical activity. This attitude, combined with the hardships of survival in the wilderness, produced an undercurrent of suspicion that all art is frivolous, and traces of this suspicion exist in America to the present day. Significantly, the first book published in British North America was religious, a collection of Psalm texts in metrical versions, the *Bay Psalm Book* (Cambridge, Mass., 1640). Less than a dozen tunes were specifically named to be used in singing these texts. The number diminished even more until finally, in the ninth edition (1698), music was included — 13 tunes from various editions of John Playford's *Brief Introduction to the Skill of Musick* (London 1666-1679).

Of the instruments that did exist in the early colonies, drums and trumpets were the most common. Mouth harps were also played and often used as barter with the Indians. Among the wealthier colonists, music apparently fared better. In 1633 inventories were made of the estates of two landholders in New Hampshire, and among the items listed are "recorders and Hoeboys," 15 of them in the first inventory and 26 in the second. Although Maypole dancing was recorded as early as 1647, no manuscript or published copies of dance music survive until the late eighteenth century. At that time the popular dances were of French and English origin — hornpipes, reels, minuets, strathspeys, marches, gavottes, allemandes, cotillions, quadrilles, and waltzes.

Black slavery was introduced to the New World early in the sixteenth century by Portuguese and Spanish traders. The English began to import their own slaves to the colonies beginning with a group of indentured servants who landed at Jamestown in 1619 and were given their freedom in 1644. Thereafter, unconditional slavery was the custom, and by 1700 it was lawful in all British colonies.

Little attention was paid to the music of slaves in those early years, but later accounts indicate that many African customs were brought over intact. Songs accompanied almost every activity—work, play, and worship. The most common form was that of the call-and-response. On Sundays and holidays, when slaves were allowed time for their own housework and gardening, they often congregated in town squares to sing and dance. A late-eighteenth-century account by a white colonist describes such a gathering: "Every voice in its highest key, in all the various languages of Africa, mixed with broken and ludicrous English, filled the air, accompanied with the music of the fiddle, tambourine, banjo, and drum."[5] Another writer claimed that the music was so "irregular and grotesque" that it defied description. However, the fact that slave music was adapted from African songs, varied and renewed to form new songs in the New World, means that some of the slave songs we know today may be the first nonaboriginal music created in North America.

Naturally, whites immediately set to work to Christianize the slaves, making them attend church services, where they sat in special pews. This and other European influences tended to regularize the phrase structure in slave music so that, for example, the solo stanzas in a call-and-response would alternate regularly with the choruses. (The colonial church practice of "lining out" a Psalm, whereby a leader sang a line that was immediately repeated by the congregation, was a closely related formal concept that probably reinforced the African call-and-response pattern and helped it survive.) European

5. Eileen Southern, *The Music of Black Americans* (New York: W. W. Norton, 1971); p. 50.

influence also had the effect of squeezing African pitch systems into diatonic scales, with perhaps one or two degrees flatted.

1720-1820[*]

The high regard for music among Africans gave them a head start in the expanding musical cultures of eighteenth-century America. Slaves who could play the flute or violin always brought high prices, and in the 1730s and 40s they were playing music from British dance collections at many of the white people's parties and dancing schools. "According to the African tradition. . .music was meant to be shared by others. . . .Consequently, the black musician was happiest when playing for the dancing and singing of others, whether white or black."[6] Sometimes the whites hired teachers to give their slaves instruction on European instruments, but almost as often the slaves taught themselves. So adept were some blacks at European music that they became teachers themselves. In 1786 a white singing-school master in New England, Andrew Law, was replaced in his job by "Frank the Negro," probably a free black.

Along with Psalm tunes and texts, which were taught to slaves all through the 1750s, a hymn repertory was gaining popularity. This began in the 1730s, when a religious movement called "The Great Awakening" swept through the colonies and created a demand for lively music. Blacks especially liked the hymns of Isaac Watts.

Throughout most of this period slaves continued to gather in city squares on holidays to sing and dance to their own music. References to the practice exist as far north as Albany. In New Orleans it occurred in Place Congo, where from 3:00 o'clock to 9:00 in the evening slaves performed large circle

6. Ibid., p. 47

dances accompanied by drums, stringed instruments (including an African exotic, the banjo), singing, and chanting. Their dancing would begin slowly and grow more and more frenzied until people began to faint. The practice was carried over into a black form of Christian worship called the "ring shout," in which the participants would shuffle slowly around a circle for hours while chanting religious texts. Even at this early date, an autonomous New World black culture was developing. The ring shout was one manifestation. Another was the African Methodist Episcopal Church, an independent black Protestant sect, which was founded in Philadelphia in 1794 and which issued the first hymnal for blacks in 1801.

In the Northern colonies, distrust of music within the Puritan sect, together with frontier hardships in general, caused music to be largely neglected among the white settlers. By the 1720s churchmen were alarmed because their congregations could sing only a few of the old Psalm tunes. Even those were now being performed in orally transmitted renditions full of embellishments considered corrupt. To correct this situation, a Massachusetts minister, John Tufts, issued a pamphlet in 1721 that contained twenty Psalm tunes in a version of staff notation that substituted letters for noteheads. It was the first American music textbook. Other such publications appeared, and singing schools and clubs arose to teach the old Psalms.

Later in the century other kinds of English church music became popular in the North—hymns (especially those by Watts) and anthems (also known as "fuguing tunes"). The latter were a model for a "New England school" of anthem composers, a group of native-born whites that included William Billings and Daniel Read. All of them, in frontier fashion, practiced many trades—tanner, storekeeper, carpenter, book publisher, horse breeder. The meager resources for instruction in America did not permit the mastery of a controlled, coordinated musical style such as was developing in Europe, so the Americans produced their own homemade music containing open fifths, "regressive" chord progressions (IV-III, III-II, etc.), disjunct voice leading, and uncoordinated textual, harmonic, and surface rhythms. Their fuguing tunes from 1770 to 1800 were five or ten-minute pieces set for four-part mixed chorus with optional instruments that doubled the voices and sometimes provided interludes. The form was a series of contrasting sections determined by the text.

In creating antipathy for British products, the American Revolution gave these New Englanders a limited vogue. Soon, however, they were outshone by professionally trained musicians from England and elsewhere, many of whom were recruited for Philadelphia and New York theaters, where music, eating, drinking, and bawdiness all mingled together in the London fashion. Some of the new arrivals not only performed, composed, gave concerts, and took pupils, but also established music shops and publishing businesses. Three examples, all from England, are Alexander Reinagle, who came in 1786; James Hewitt, who came in 1792; and Benjamin Carr, who came in 1793. Reinagle, whose piano sonatas are reminiscent of C. P. E. Bach, was music director and composer for theaters in Philadelphia. Hewitt occupied similar positions in New York and Boston. Carr, a singer in ballad operas, established a publishing business and music shop in Philadelphia and, along with his father and brother, extended the business to Baltimore and New York.

The music published by these and other men was intended mostly for amateurs to use at home. It consisted of "martial and patriotic music, opera airs and traditional [English, Scotch, and Irish] songs, dance tunes, and a smattering of programmatic or absolute instrumental music."[7] *A Collection of the Most Favorite Country Dances*, published by Hewitt in

7. H. Wiley Hitchcock, *Music in the United States: A Historical Introduction*, (Englewood Cliffs, N.J.: Prentice Hall, Inc., 1964), p. 27.

1802, contains "lusty, ongoing fiddle tunes, patterning along in running eighth-notes until, at the phrase endings, they land stompingly on repeated cadence chords."[8] Programmatic battle pieces, especially Franz Kotzwara's *The Battle of Prague*, were published again and again. Mozart, Haydn, Handel, Beethoven, and Weber were the most popular of the great Europeans.

It was inevitable that this influx of music and musicians from Europe would have both good and bad effects on the new nation. It served to build vigorous concert and publishing businesses in the Eastern cities, but it also shattered the musical self-confidence of Americans. Almost a century was needed to rebuild this confidence, and even today many Americans believe that Europeans are still the better producers and judges of fine music.

In the South the pattern of life for whites was somewhat gentler than in the North, at least among those segments of the population that have been studied. The growth of large plantations based on slave labor permitted the accumulation of wealth and leisure, and the diaries of plantation families, with their descriptions of music lessons, home concerts, and parties lasting three or four days, could have been written from a country estate in England or France. Many of America's early political leaders came from this environment: George Washington, who was a patron of music; Thomas Jefferson, who was a violinist; Francis Hopkinson, the Philadelphia lawyer who claimed that his songs from the late 1750s were the first music written by a "native" of the United States. (Benjamin Franklin, born in Boston, proves that a gentleman amateur could also come from the North; however, the type was less common there until later in the century.) Manuscript music collections made in Southern homes during this period contain songs from ballad operas as well as instrumental works (usually

8. Ibid., p. 36.

in keyboard transcription) by Handel, Corelli, Stamitz, Galuppi, and others popular in England and France.

During the first half of the century the coastal city of Charleston, S.C., was the main point of entry for professional musicians. The first ballad opera in America was performed there in 1735. However, the first city to have grand opera was New Orleans. In 1796, when the company was established, the city's population was only 12,000, yet by the 1805-06 season there was enough interest in opera to support a repertory of works by Monsigny, Grétry, Dalayrac, Boieldieu, Méhul, and Paisiello. During 1827-1833 the company went on tour, presenting the first grand opera to be seen in Boston, Philadelphia, and Baltimore.

During the second half of the eighteenth century a new religious revival from England took root in the South and later in the North. Its chief leaders, John and Charles Wesley, emphasized an emotional experience of personal salvation in which vigorous hymn singing played a prominent role. After 1800 it was common for revival camp meetings to be held in the South. Tents accommodating 3,000-5,000 people would be set up in the woods, and people would gather for four or five days to picnic, sing, and pray. The music at these gatherings is preserved in such collections as *Kentucky Harmony* (1816), *Missouri Harmony* (1820), and *Southern Harmony* (1835), which contain eighteenth-century tunes from New England, Scotland, and Ireland, and some new pieces as well. Blacks often attended the meetings, where they lived in segregated quarters. With their customary inventiveness, they developed a repertory of their own, spirituals, which are a blend of African and camp-meeting songs.

1820-1920

Concurrent with the rise of major cities in the East and Midwest, primitive settlements were still being established along the Western frontiers. And concurrent with the development of an educated and wealthy merchant class in the cities, millions of unskilled and uneducated laborers from Europe and Asia were arriving to take up life in the poorest sections of every town. Nineteenth-century immigrants tended not to blend with their fellows from other countries nor with the existing population. Instead, many of them remained as they had been in the Old Country, forming ethnic pockets that preserved the language, food, customs, and music of their homelands. (Only one such group seems to have existed in the eighteenth century, the Moravians, who farmed in North Carolina and Pennsylvania and made Central European music together.) Thus the pattern of stratified cultures and musics, which had begun to emerge in the eighteenth century, became increasingly pronounced and variegated in the nineteenth. Only recently has the full diversity of cultures in nineteeth-century America been appreciated and studied, and therefore only a few highlights of nineteenth-century music in the U.S. can be described here.

Upper and middle-class urban residents consumed a great deal of salon music, mostly European in origin but without such difficult repertories as the piano music of Chopin and the more dramatic songs of Schubert. The British singer Henry Russell, who toured the U.S. during 1833-1841, wrote one of the most popular pieces of the time, *The Old Arm Chair*. The song "is quite simple, the melodic style essentially declamatory, in easy 4/4 rhythms, with an occasional touch of affective chromaticism and a climactic, shuddering diminished-seventh chord. The form is strophic. The most frequent harmonic progression is the gentle I-IV-I, often made even softer by a tonic pedalpoint. . . .Most characteristic of the melodic method are the many sighing, dropping appoggiaturas."[9] Easy, sentimental songs of this type were used both at home and in concert; in the latter case they alternated with excerpts from European symphonic and chamber works.

One of America's most famous composers, Stephen Foster, grew up in this sort of environment near Pittsburgh, Pa. His songs until the late 1840s were bland in the Russell manner, after which he borrowed the musical and speech inflections of blacks and created dozens of memorable pieces such as *Old Folks At Home, Oh! Susanna,* and *Camptown Races.* Louis Moreau Gottschalk, born into a wealthy New Orleans family, was another composer of the time who owed his originality to non-European sources. Although his family sent him to Paris at age twelve to study piano and composition, his musical borrowings from blacks, Cubans, and other Latin Americans whom he had heard as a child gave his music its zest. His popularity in Europe during 1845-1853 rivaled that of Chopin, but at home he did not have a comparable success until his last grand tour in 1862. Perhaps the novelty-prone audiences he played for in Europe had led him to create music that was too startling for the less sophisticated American public.

Nineteenth-century hymns and anthems in the Northern cities were mostly adaptations of Giardini, Purcell, Handel, Burney, and other dead Europeans. In the hymn collections of Lowell Mason this tendency to venerate the past turned into an application of late-eighteenth-century harmony and voice leading so rigid that it often ruled out an interesting melody. Highly sentimental Gospel hymns from later in the century derive from this style and perhaps also from that of the German *Volkslied.* Only in rural areas, especially in the South, were

9. Ibid., p. 59.

vigorous, folk-based hymns still sung. "These songs were Irish, Scotch, and English. . . .They were the common possession of early Americans of those ethnic stocks—those people who never left the [coastal regions of the South], those who came into the highlands and settled there, and those greater numbers who trekked through the mountain gaps, down the western slopes, and spread into the rolling country and plains."[10] So stratified had American cultures become by now that the existence of old folk hymns, though they were sung by hundreds of thousands of devotees in holiday festivals from Virginia to Texas, was virtually unknown to academics, urban businessmen, and concert musicians until the 1930s.

Ballad opera, which was a staple of eighteenth-century city life, was replaced in the nineteenth century by an American creation, the minstrel show. From early in the century white actors in England and America had blackened their faces and portrayed black characters in plays. Variety acts in blackface began to appear in American cities in the 1830s, and in 1842 and 1843 small casts of white entertainers in Buffalo and New York presented full-length, coordinated, blackface minstrel shows. The typical show had two acts and lasted an hour and a half. The first act consisted of jokes, songs, and repartee in black dialect, with all of the performers seated in a semicircle on stage and dressed as stock characters. The second act was a variety show with a grand finale. The standard instrumentation included bone castanets, banjo, violin, and tambourine, to which an accordion, another banjo, winds, and more percussion might be added. By the 1860s there were thirty full-time companies touring the countryside with as many as thirty to forty performers each. In the morning they paraded through town in costume and gave a free outdoor concert of overtures and medleys. At night they gave their show. Although

10. George Pullen Jackson, *Spiritual Folk-Songs of Early America*, 2d ed. (Locust Valley, N.Y.: J. J. Augustin, 1953), p. 1.

some of the dance tunes they used were Irish or Scotch in origin, the syncopation and irregular rhythmic stresses showed the influence of black performance styles. It was for minstrel shows of the 1850s that Foster wrote his most beloved songs and for which Dan Emmett wrote the most famous song in America, *Dixie*. After the Civil War black minstrel companies began to appear (the blacks often in blackface), and a black composer, James Bland, took Foster's place as the leading writer of minstrel songs. The genre began to decline in the 1870s, and after 1900 it was replaced as a popular entertainment by vaudeville and operetta.

The appearance of black entertainers in some minstrel companies — as well as the minstrel show itself — indicates that aspects of black culture were beginning to have commercial value in the white world. Most of the other important contacts between whites and blacks took place in Southern cities, where blacks continued to play European music at white balls and where, in New Orleans, a Negro Philharmonic Society was formed in the 1830s to give formal concerts of European music. Blacks also had their own brass bands for street processions and, where permitted, gathered in taverns and danced to orchestras of fiddles, flutes, clarinets, triangles, tambourines, and drums.[11] African dance and music were still being performed in Place Congo.

It was in this lively atmosphere that blacks in New Orleans conceived the first of several new styles, ragtime. Before the Civil War, instrumental music among slaves had consisted typically of tunes on fiddles and banjos accompanied by foot stomping and knee patting. In the 1880s this sound texture was transferred to the piano. "In piano-rag music, the left hand took over the task of stomping and patting while the right hand performed syncopated melodies, using motives reminiscent of

11. Southern, *The Music of Black Americans*, p. 138.

fiddle and banjo tunes."[12] Whereas the layered treatment of rhythm derived from African sources, the instrumentation and harmony were European, as were the tempo and form, which derived from multi-sectional dances and marches. Large numbers of white people first learned of the style at the Chicago World's Fair in 1893, which attracted many rag pianists to the city, including Scott Joplin, then in his mid-twenties. A few years later ragtime was introduced to white society in the Eastern cities. It had an unsettling effect on many people — comparable to the effect Elvis Presley had in the 1950s — yet for the first decade of the new century it was the country's most popular music.

A second composite style, blues, evolved during 1900-1910, primarily in the taverns and brothels of New Orleans, Chicago, and New York. The blues has roots in the mournful songs of black stevedores and farm slaves. The form is usually a-a'-b with a syncopated melody moving over duple-meter chording in the bass (as in ragtime). The most distinctive feature, the performance style, is African. It makes use of scoops, slides, whining, and growling sounds (often transferred to instruments), all of which are foreign to European standards of vocal production. The scale pattern includes irregular inflections of the third, fifth, and seventh degrees, and sometimes the sixth. Even more important is the role of the performer. "It is an aural music, intended to take on its shape and style during the performance. The notation of a blues gives only an approximation of how it may sound."[13] This view of performance is different from ornamentation in the European manner, for the true shape of a blues is dependent on textures of performed sound that are nowhere indicated in the printed score. The performer is co-composer.

12. Ibid., p. 313.
13. Ibid., p. 333.

A third composite style was jazz. Its first phase, now known as Dixieland, was a fusion of street-band instrumentation, blues performance practice, and ragtime principles of syncopation over a steady bass. Although jazz developed among blacks, it was introduced to the country at large by white bands from New Orleans, first in Chicago (1915) and then in New York (1917). In Europe, however, black musicians fighting in World War I were the first people to bring jazz to white audiences.

During the latter half of the nineteenth century the European concert tradition expanded in American cities, establishing a network of institutions that maintained a vigorous life until the 1960s. Great impetus in this development came from the tours of foreign virtuosos: the violinist Ole Bull beginning in 1843, the pianist Leopold de Meyer in 1845-1847, the soprano Jenny Lind in 1850, and the conductor Louis Antoine Jullien, who in 1853 brought forty musicians from London, augmented them with sixty Americans, and gave concerts in New York. That Jenny Lind's tour was managed by a circus promoter, P. T. Barnum, is perhaps a uniquely American juxtaposition of arts.

Conservatories for the training of native talent developed during the 1860s in Baltimore, Oberlin, Boston, Cincinnati, and Chicago. Early in the twentieth century other schools were founded in New York, San Francisco, Rochester, and Philadelphia. Orchestras were founded: New York (1842), Boston (1881), Chicago (1891), Cincinnati (1895), Philadelphia (1900), Minneapolis (1903), San Francisco (1911), Detroit (1914), Cleveland (1918), and Los Angeles (1919). Only two major opera companies were formed during these years, the Metropolitan (1883) and the Chicago (1910-1932); the San Francisco Opera followed in 1923. Finally, major publishing houses were established in Boston, New York, and Philadelphia.

Nineteenth-century concert music by native composers followed European leads. Thus, the mid-century overtures, symphonies, and operas of William Henry Fry have been compared to Auber and Bellini, and those of George Frederick Bristow, to Mendelssohn. Then, in the 1880s, a new school of composers emerged in New England led by John Knowles Paine, George Chadwick, and Horatio Parker. They had all been trained in Germany, and they became active here in universities and conservatories. Edward MacDowell occupied a similar position in the musical life of New York. Charles T. Griffes emerged after the turn of the century and was the product more of French and Russian taste than of German. In the late 1910s, toward the end of his brief life, he was experimenting with Asian subjects and instrumental effects, a harbinger of things to come. The Russian influence at the turn of the century helped stimulate a nationalist trend in the U.S. (emphasizing Indian and black musics), of which Arthur Farwell was the principal leader. Significantly, he came from the Midwest and was not associated with the Germanic group in the North-east. Only one black composer gained national recognition in the concert field, Harry T. Burleigh, the nationslist who introduced Negro spirituals to Dvořák during the latter's visit of 1892-1895.

Though they were never regarded by the social elite as a major cultural institution, band concerts became very popular. One of America's most famous composers, John Philip Sousa, became leader of the Marine Band in 1880 and of his own ensemble in 1892. His exuberant music seems to reflect the satisfied feelings that many Americans had about the progress of their country. A more innovative band composer, the black musician Jim Europe, formed an all-black band during World War I that became a sensation on the Continent. Although the group did not improvise in performance, it did borrow such jazz instrumental features as mutes, novel tonguing, a pinched embouchure, and syncopated rhythmic stresses. Further brilliance resulted from the fact that Europe's arrangements were in ten to twelve distinct parts in the symphonic manner, instead of only four as was customary in Sousa's music.

Since 1900

Beginning with Charles Ives, white composers in the U.S. produced music that became a seminal influence in Western concert circles. (Black Americans, of course, were already producing seminal music in blues and jazz.) Ives was a new kind of composer, prefigured to some extent by Wagner, who not only writes a startling new music but invents its theoretical foundation and stylistic conventions; who may also create new sound sources, new performing environments, and new notations; and who, during his lifetime, usually attracts only a small and specialized audience. Others in American concert music who typify this independence include Edgard Varèse, Henry Cowell, Harry Partch, John Cage, Milton Babbitt, and many of the younger composers who came to prominence in the 1960s.

The immediate causes for the appearance of this type of composer have not been investigated, but the following factors were undoubtedly important in the U.S.: By 1900 there were good educational facilities, an ever-rising level of prosperity, and a growing sense of national well-being, all of which contributed to a sense of cultural independence from Europe. The close proximity of different musical cultures probably suggested to many individuals that they too might assemble musical systems of their own. Added to this was the exuberant sense of a country still expanding and the American tradition of reckless individualism, expressed most strikingly in the lives of many industrialists, frontiersmen, and outlaws.

Although Ives has become a prominent force in music only since the early 1950s, most of his music dates from before 1920. His father was a musical experimenter who instilled in Ives an ability to listen to musical sounds without blocking out or mentally justifying such factors as wrong notes, out-of-tune instruments, and noise. Ives's innovations probably resulted both from his ability to hear the true qualities of sounds and sound conglomerates and from a freedom of mind that allowed him to permit forms and shapes to grow organically from the unique properties of the sounds he was working with. It is also important that he did not earn his living from music and thus was not bound economically to the accepted standards of his day.

Varese, who moved from Europe to New York in 1915, was a skilled choral and orchestral conductor, and he took a leading role in avant-garde activities of the 1920s. This marked the first blossoming of New York as an international music center. The period "was one of extensive exploration in American music, and the intensity and importance of the activity has scarcely any parallel in the European music of the time. . . . Ideas such as tone clusters, new scalar and rhythmic formations, new notations, new instruments, and especially, new mechanical techniques were very much in the air."[14] Like Ives, Varese imagined musical sound differently from other composers. "Indeed, the real subject matter of this music is texture, color, accent, and dynamic. . . . The materials consist of fixed, invented musical shapes, powerful, static blocks of sound piled up in great, spatial juxtapositions."[15] The Great Depression forced a halt to most experimental music activity in public, and Varèse could not continue to exert leadership. During the 1950s, however, his music came back into public consciousness and he made significant new contributions, this time in the field of tape music.

Cowell became active in New York music in the late 1920s. He had grown up in San Francisco, with its large

14. Eric Salzman, *Twentieth-Century Music: An Introduction* (Englewood Cliffs, N.J.: Prentice-Hall, Inc., 1967), p. 148.
15. Ibid., p. 150.

Asian populations, and in rural areas of Kansas, Oklahoma, and Iowa, where folk music was a living tradition. These early influences acted on his fertile and inquisitive mind, producing a wide range of innovations. As early as 1912 he invented the tone cluster. Beginning in 1923 he began making piano sounds directly on the strings. In the 1930s he began using indeterminacy.

The early influences on Cowell demonstrate that the Western regions of the country were now becoming sources for new musical ideas. This is dramatically illustrated in Harry Partch, also born in California, who stayed in the West working at odd jobs, teaching himself about music, and developing his own theory of pitch and harmony, his own instruments, and his own conception of performance. His work proceeded through the 1930s but did not reach a wide public until the mid-1940s.

At the same time that America's musical consciousness was being pricked by the avant-garde, other and broader strata of the country's music were becoming known. For example, a new folk-song repertory, cowboy ballads, was found to have developed in the West. In the latter half of the nineteenth century "the cowboys were shut off from the rest of the world as few other modern workers have been. In the close-knit little community that they formed they shared food, experiences, and thoughts. Thus it happened that. . . .the old, old conditions for the creation of folk song were reset."[16] The American Folklore Society, which had been founded in 1888, began intensive field work in the 1920s. The first book of George Pullen Jackson on white folk hymns in the South appeared in 1933. Record companies discovered the "black" market and

---

16. Alvis D. Carlson, "Cowboy Ballads At Our Firesides," originally published in 1931; reprinted in Linnell Gentry, ed., *A History and Encyclopedia of Country, Western, and Gospel Music*, 2d ed. (Nashville, Tenn.: Clairmont Corp., 1969), p. 20.

issued millions of "race records" designed specifically for black audiences. Record producers began making trips through the South to record both white and black folk musicians (whom they paid $25 each). On word that such a scout was nearby, "homemade fiddles are dusted off, mandolins and guitars are taken off the shelf, as well as. . .washboards, piepans, automobile horns, cowbells, train whistles, jew's harps, combs, kazoos, harmonicas, sweet-potato fifes, and carpenter's saws."[17] Much later, in the 1950s, the assorted cultures in the industrial cities began to be recognized and enjoyed as well. In Pittsburgh, for example, an annual folk festival was founded in 1957 to display the national music, dance, handicrafts, and food of the city's population. The nationalities represented in 1972 were Bulgaria, Croatia, Denmark, Egypt, England, Ghana, Greece, Hungary, India, Ireland, Israel, Italy, Latvia, Lebanon, Lithuania, the Philippines, Poland, Russia, Scotland, Serbia, Slovakia, Slovenia, and the Ukraine.

This expanded view of America's identity was reflected in nationalist concert music of the 1920s to 1940s. Even though he lived in Paris most of these years, Virgil Thomson quoted from early American hymnody. One of Cowell's novelties was a series called *Hymn and Fuguing Tunes* (1944-1964). Roy Harris quoted folk tunes and also suggested through harmonic and rhythmic means a feeling of spaciousness that came to be labeled American. The internal cross-rhythms and ambiguous meters in many of his melodies are typical of the country's folk music, and one of the themes in his *Third Symphony* is "very chromatic, uncertainly focused on any single tonic note; fluid in tempo, phrase-length, meter, and dynamics but even-paced in rhythm, it seems boundless, a grand rhetorical prose-like utterance."[18] The widely spaced sonorities in ballet and

17. Maurice Zolotow, "Hillbilly Boom," originally published in 1944; reprinted in Gentry, *History and Encyclopedia. . .*, p. 38.

18. Hitchcock, *Music in the United States*, p. 206.

film music by Aaron Copland, combined with folk-tune quotations and national subjects, also came to be identified as American. He and many others used aspects of the jazz idiom as well.

As the nationalist trend gained momentum it joined forces with the neoclassic movement from France, now the preferred country of American composers who studied in Europe. The reintroduction of familiar and accessible materials, which neoclassicism encouraged, was compatible with the use of folk sources. The composite result from 1930 through the 1940s was a less explosive music than had appeared in the 1920s. There were, of course, exceptions, such as Copland's *Piano Variations* (1930), but the music most readily identified with this period includes the early works of Roger Sessions, Elliott Carter, Arthur Berger, and Lukas Foss and a large segment of the output of Copland, Harris, Thomson, Walter Piston, William Schuman, Irving Fine, and David Diamond. Some of the New Englanders who had come to prominence in the 1880s were still productive; they and composers like Howard Hanson and Samuel Barber kept alive a more romantic, nineteenth-century tradition, sometimes combined with nationalist features.

After World War I jazz spread outward from New Orleans. In 1920 the Creole Jazz Band of King Oliver went to Chicago, and other cities also became important jazz centers, especially Kansas City, Detroit, New York, and Memphis. New sub-styles evolved. Boogie-woogie, a two-tiered bass-and-melody piano style based on blues, arose in Chicago in the early 1920s and was further developed in nightclubs in Harlem. In the early 1930s a Kansas City style evolved out of local conditions there, which were determined by the city's position at the hub of river, rail, and highway networks. Musicians stopping by used the blues, a commonly held tradition, as the basis for jam sessions in which any number of players could join. The underlying rhythm was a steady succession of beats but without the march-like stresses of New Orleans Dixieland. After a session began, the players took turns at solo improvisations, a format that permitted strangers to share and compete with each other. Riffs were introduced, short melodic-rhythmic ideas repeated ostinatolike at the beginning of a piece and as background to the improvisatory sections. Count Basie formed his band in Kansas City at this time.

The era of big bands, which were centered in New York, followed from about 1930 to 1950. Black bandleaders, such as Louis Armstrong, Jelly Roll Morton, and Duke Ellington found ways to combine big-band orchestrations with solo and collective improvisation, thus retaining some of the concepts of spontaneous performance that had characterized the early years of jazz. White band leaders such as Paul Whiteman, Glenn Miller, Tommy Dorsey, and Benny Goodman preferred a smoother, more controlled style. Their music became better known than that of blacks, partly because the American public was then more responsive to a gentler approach and partly because whites had easier access to radio stations, recording companies, film studios, and newspaper reporters.

The style known as bop or bebop arose in Harlem nightclubs in the early 1940s, led by such black musicians as trumpeter Dizzy Gillespie, pianist Thelonious Monk, and double bassist Charlie Mingus. Improvisation again came to the fore. In a reversal of texture, the double bass and bass drum became solo instruments, and the reiteration of a steady beat was transferred to the top cymbal. The electric guitar now became a principal sustaining instrument.

In some varieties of the style called hard bop, irregular, nonmelodic jabs and slashes of sound created extremely dissonant rhythms and harmonies. This jazz, epitomized by the music of saxophonist Charlie Parker, was not danceable. It was an experimental chamber music meant for listening. A "new thing" in jazz evolved in the late 1950s under the leadership of saxophonists John Coltrane and Ornette Coleman, who largely dispensed with tonality, meter, melody, and pre-existent materials and created a style based primarily on texture.

The black rural music recorded for race records of the 1940s came to be known as "rhythm and blues." This style was copied by white musicians in the 1950s, most notably Elvis Presley, and renamed rock 'n' roll. Its unyielding pulse, its loudness, and the flamboyant style of its performers revolutionized the commercial white popular-music scene. Very shortly a more sophisticated style called rock evolved, and hundreds of rock groups appeared, the most famous being the Beatles from England. They used complex techniques of electronic sound production, amplification, and distortion. Surprisingly they remained commercially successful even though in the concert world most audiences found such techniques unacceptable. Rock engendered a culture of its own. It marked the first time in modern Western history that music was an essential element in the lives of a large segment of the white population. It motivated hundreds of thousands of young people to learn an instrument (usually the guitar), to perform, and even to compose.[19] Pete Seeger, Bob Dylan, Joan Baez, and others developed a simpler and quieter solo style called folk or folk-rock, which borrowed some features from the traditional folk ballad.

Also on the popular front, the incorporation of ragtime elements into the operetta after World War I initiated a trend that culminated in the Broadway musical, a genre created not by individual composers but by teams of writers, lyricists, arrangers, and orchestrators, along with singers, directors, and producers, according to predictions and formulas

19. Charles A. Reich, *The Greening of America*, paperback ed. (New York: Bantam Books, 1971), p. 262.

of audience response. The vitality of the genre in its heyday is indicated by the fact that although Americans have written hundreds of operas, only one work has entered the world operatic repertory, Gershwin's musical *Porgy and Bess.*

Many general historians remember the 1950s in America as an uneventful time. Politically uneventful it may have been, but in the arts it was one of the country's most exciting decades. All of the musical institutions that had been established in the preceding century were flourishing. To this was added the long-playing high-fidelity record, which created a major new outlet for music as well as new audiences. Universities had now become significant patrons of music, providing jobs and facilities for hundreds of composers and performers. The rise of Nazism in Europe had brought most of the century's leading composers to the U.S. (Bartók, Hindemith, Krenek, Martinů, Milhaud, Schoenberg, Stravinsky, Weill, and Wolpe). All of these conditions transformed the U.S. into the nerve center of concert music, a world role that lasted until the late 1950s, when economic recovery from World War II, a lessening of Cold War restrictions on the exchange of ideas, an increasing diversity of accepted styles, and better world communications dissolved the national boundaries of musical leadership.

The decade of the 1950s was marked by far-reaching innovations in the work of U.S. composers. Milton Babbitt was already extending Schoenberg's 12-tone method into a comprehensive serial system. Elliott Carter was abandoning the stereotypes of musical structure and building each new work on some principle of its own derived from properties inherent in its sound materials. John Cage began in 1950 to work with principles of indeterminacy and in 1951-52 with tape music. In 1952 Otto Luening and Vladimir Ussachevsky founded the Columbia-Princeton Electronic Music Center. In 1952-53 Earle Brown and Morton Feldman introduced mobile or open form and graphic notation. In 1953 Henry Brant began developing-principles of spatial orchestration. Additional energy came from the past achievements of Ives and Partch, which were now becoming known, and from Varèse, who was composing his last works.

These progressive trends of the 1950s were not immediately taken up by the majority of concert composers. The norm was neoclassicism and later, in the 1960s, a contrapuntal, atonal (usually 12-tone) music with generally nonrepetitive phrase structure. However, despite the prevalence of these normative styles, a widespread shift to avant-garde thinking began to occur in the mid-1960s. In the work of many younger composers texture became the dominant element in the musical hierarchy. In some cases a collagelike joining of disparate sounds and musics was attempted. Improvisation and collective composition gained appeal. The philosophies and sound ideals of Asia entered people's consciousness, as did the aesthetics and performance practice of jazz. Nontempered pitch structures and nonpitched sounds were absorbed into the realm of musical sound. New sound sources and instrumental techniques were tested. The possibilities of minimal changes in sound flow were investigated. Electronic apparatus, and later the computer, extended the creative and controlling power over sound. The resources of film, light, video, movement, and amplified sound were giving rise to a new theater genre, multimedia. To all this was added the domestic turmoil (primarily racial) that erupted in the mid-1960s and the massive hatred aroused by the racial integration programs of Lyndon Johnson and his decision to expand the Vietnam War, both of which drove many composers to new, intense, even painful levels of expression.

(Sadly, most critics, professional musicians, and audiences found new music a dismal thing or, if they had a sense of humor, an inconsequential bit of neodadaism. In what now seems partly an effort to halt change and rebuild the past, the hierarchy of the nation — city, state, and federal governments, universities, foundations, and corporations — constructed grandiose performing arts centers to house the old-guard orchestras, operas, and recitalists. However, the large audiences needed to pay the upkeep of these halls did not stay beyond a few seasons, and by the mid-1970s even the Metropolitan Opera had to advertise in the subways and sell tickets on credit.)

Since the early 1970s an increasing number of composers have assimilated the innovations of the 1950s and 60s. This is true not only in the U.S., of course, but across the globe. Also, an increasing number of composers are once again talking about critical standards, something rarely discussed among innovators ten or twenty years ago. Future developments seem to hover between two extremes: the possibility that some sort of new "common practice" is at hand, and the possibility that widely varying points of view will continue to proliferate, each of them attracting its own audience.

October 1972-January 1973
(revised May 1975)

Remembrance of Things Past: The Concerto for Orchestra

Among the notable contributions that the seventeenth and eighteenth centuries made to Western concert music were the several instrumental and vocal genres that remained in vogue for the next two centuries. Not until the dissolution of neoclassicism did their usefulness to innovative composers wear out. The nineteenth century contributed a few additional genres, mostly of a programmatic nature, such as the lied and chanson, the tone poem, and the character piece for piano. By comparison our own century has been the great destroyer. With amazing swiftness its innovators have thrown aside first one and then another convention until finally nothing has remained that is sturdy enough to build the old edifices. Music itself has lived on, of course, and with an exuberance beyond anything we have known before, but nowadays it seems to have few commonly accepted building materials and no commonly accepted architecture.

This description of our century has one exception, a limited one, in the concerto for orchestra. Born of neoclassicism

This essay was published in *Notes* (U.S.) 30, no. 1 (September 1973). Reprinted by permission.

it represents both a quintessential nostalgia and a consummate integration of historical elements: the nineteenth-century orchestra, the eighteenth-century symphony, and the seventeenth-century concerto. So captivating is this idea that over the last fifty years it has attracted composers from Europe, Russia, North and South America, and Japan. Already, however, it seems to be on the wane.

My own work in twentieth-century music has not encompassed a detailed study of this genre. Yet, enough information has turned up to call attention to its existence and to encourage others to use it. The following list contains the concertos I know about, organized by date of composition. My criterion for inclusion is semantic rather than stylistic. If a composer has called his work a concerto, I have noted it. To me his use of the term implies an identification with a unique twentieth-century genre, and it was this feeling of community that first intrigued me about the subject. More thorough studies should be able to amplify my list considerably and point up the many overlappings and cross-relations that exist with other works.[1]

Checklist of Concertos for Orchestra

Composer	Opus number, title, special instrumentation, other information	Publisher or distributor
	1925	
Paul Hindemith (Germany, 1895-1963)	Op. 38, Concerto for Orchestra	B. Schott, Mainz
	1927	
Giorgio Ghedini (Italy, 1892-1965)	Concerto Grosso for Orchestra	Suvini-Zerboni, Milan

1. A good place to begin in making comparisons is Casella's *Concerto for String Quartet* (1923-24), which antedates the first item in my list.

1928

Jerzy Fitelberg (Poland-U.S., 1903-1951)	Concerto for String Orchestra	Universal, Vienna
Ildebrando Pizzetti (Italy, 1880-1968)	Concerto Dell'Estate for Orchestra	G. Ricordi, Milan

1929

Nikos Skalkottas (Greece, 1904-1949)	Concerto for Wind Orchestra	unpublished

1930

Gösta Nystroem (Sweden, 1890-1966)	Concerto for String Orchestra [No. 1 of 2]	Nordiska, Stockholm

1931

Sándor Jemnitz (Hungary, 1890-1963)	Concerto for Chamber Orchestra [No. 1 of 2]	unpublished
Gian Francesco Malipiero (Italy, 1882-)	Concerti per Orchestra	G. Ricordi, Milan

1933

Walter Piston (U.S., 1894-)	Concerto for Orchestra	Associated, New York

1933-1934

Goffredo Petrassi (Italy, 1904-)	Concerto for Orchestra [No. 1 of 7]	G. Ricordi, Milan

1935

Wolfgang Fortner (Germany, 1907-)	Concerto for String Orchestra	B. Schott, Mainz

1936

Michał Kondracki (Poland-U.S., 1902-)	Concerto for Orchestra	unpublished

1937

Alfredo Casella (Italy, 1883-1947)	Concerto for Orchestra	G. Ricordi, Milan
Daniel Ruyneman (Holland, 1886-1963)	Concerto for Orchestra	unpublished

1937-1938

Igor Stravinsky (Russia-U.S., 1882-1971)	Concerto in E Flat for Chamber Orchestra, [No. 1 of 2], "Dumbarton Oaks Concerto"	B. Schott, Mainz

1938

Bohuslav Martinů
(Czechoslovakia, 1890-
1959)

Concerto Grosso for Orchestra

Universal, Vienna

1938-1939

Michael Tippett
(England, 1905-)

Concerto for Double String
Orchestra [No. 1 of 2]

B. Schott, Mainz

1939

Zoltán Kodály
(Hungary, 1882-1967)

Concerto for Orchestra

Editio Musica
Budapest

Petro Petridis
(Greece, 1892-)

Concerto for String Orchestra

unpublished

1940

David Diamond
(U.S., 1915-)

Concerto for Small Orchestra

Southern, New
York

Giorgio Ghedini
(Italy, 1892-1965)

Concerto for Orchestra,
"Architettura"

G. Ricordi, Milan

Robert Palmer
(U.S., 1915-)

Concerto for Small Orchestra
[No. 1 of 2]
(withdrawn by the composer)

unpublished

1941

Ellis Kohs
(U.S., 1916-)

Concerto for Orchestra

American Com-
posers Alliance,
New York

1943

Béla Bartók
(Hungary, 1881-1945)

Concerto for Orchestra

Boosey and
Hawkes, New York

Robert Palmer
(U.S., 1915-)

Concerto for Orchestra
[No. 2 of 2]
(withdrawn by the composer)

unpublished

1944

Hans Chemin-Petit
(Germany, 1902-)

Concerto for Orchestra

R. Lienau, Berlin

Morton Gould
(U.S., 1913-)

Concerto for Orchestra

Mills,
c/o Belwin-Mills,
New York

Tadeusz Kassern
(Poland, 1904-1957)

Concerto for String Orchestra

Polskie
Wydawnictwo
Muzyczny, Warsaw

Stjepan Šulek
(Yugoslavia, 1914-)

Classical Concerto for Orchestra

Universal, Vienna

1945

Ingvar Lidhold (Sweden, 1921-)	Concerto for String Orchestra	C. Gehrman, Stockholm
Miklos Rozsa (Hungary-U.S., 1907-)	Concerto for String Orchestra	unpublished

1946

Hilding Rosenberg (Sweden, 1892-)	Concerto for String Orchestra [No. 1 of 2]	Nordiska, Stockholm
Igor Stravinsky (Russia-U.S., 1882-1971)	Concerto in D for String Orchestra [No. 2 of 2], "Basle Concerto"	Boosey and Hawkes, New York

1947

Raymond Chevreuille (Belgium, 1901-)	Op. 37, Concerto for Orchestra	Centre Belge de Documentation Musicale, Brussels
Guido Turchi (Italy, 1916-)	Concerto Breve for Strings	Suvini-Zerboni, Milan

1948

Harald Genzmer (Germany, 1909-)	Concerto in C for Orchestra [No. 1 of 2]	B. Schott, Mainz
Viktor Kalabis (Czechoslovakia, 1923-)	Concerto for Chamber Orchestra [No. 1 of 2], "Hommage à Stravinsky"	unpublished
Ferenc Szabó (Hungary, 1902-1969)	Concerto for Orchestra, "Hazatérés" ["Homecoming"]	Editio Musica Budapest
Bernd Alois Zimmermann (Germany, 1918-1970)	Concerto for String Orchestra	unpublished

1949

Bernhard Heiden (Germany-U.S., 1910-)	Concerto for Small Orchestra	Associated, New York
Lazar Nikolov (Bulgaria, 1922-)	Concerto for String Orchestra	Union of Bulgarian Composers, Sophia
Alan Rawsthorne (England, 1905-1970)	Concerto for String Orchestra	Oxford, London
Hilding Rosenberg (Sweden, 1892-)	Concerto for Orchestra [No. 2 of 2]	unpublished

1949-1950

Antonio Estévez (Venezuela, 1916-)	Concierto Homenaje a José Angel Lamas	unpublished

1950

Everett Helm (U S., 1913-)	Concerto for String Orchestra	Alkor, Cassel
Harold Shapero (U.S., 1920-)	Concerto for Orchestra	unpublished

1950-1954

Witold Lutosławski (Poland, 1913-)	Concerto for Orchestra	Polskie Wydawnictwo Muzyczne, Warsaw

1951

Nicolai Berezowski (Russia-U.S., 1900-1953)	Sextet Concerto for String Orchestra	Associated, New York
Alan Hovhaness (U.S., 1911-)	Concerto for Orchestra, "Arevakal"	Associated, New York
Otto Luéning (U.S., 1900-)	Kentucky Concerto for Orchestra	Highgate, c/o Galaxy, New York
Goffredo Petrassi (Italy, 1904-)	Concerto for Orchestra [No. 2 of 7]	Suvini-Zerboni, Milan

1952

Bruno Bartolozzi (Italy, 1911-)	Concerto for Orchestra	Suvini-Zerboni, Milan

1953

Tadeusz Baird (Poland, 1928-)	Concerto for Orchestra	Polskie Wydawnictwo Muzycyne, Warsaw
Jacques Ibert (France, 1890-1962)	Louisville Concerto for Orchestra	A. Leduc, Paris
Goffredo Petrassi (Italy, 1904-)	Concerto for Orthcestra [No. 3 of 7], "Récréation concertante"	Suvini-Zerboni, Milan
Andrei Volkonsky (U.S.S.R., 1933-)	Concerto for Orchestra	unpublished

1953-1954

S.C. Eckhardt-Gramatté (Russia-Canada, 1902-)	Concerto for Orchestra	Canadian Music Center, Toronto
Yorgo Sicilianos (Greece, 1922-)	Op. 12, Concerto for Orchestra	Greek Ministry of Education, Athens

1954

Sándor Jemnitz (Hungary, 1890-1963)	Concerto for String Orchestra [No. 2 of 2]	unpublished
Yannis A. Papaïoannou (Greece, 1910-)	Concerto for Orchestra	Edition Modern, Munich

Goffredo Petrassi (Italy, 1904-)	Concerto for String Orchestra [No. 4 of 7]	Suvini-Zerboni, Milan
Endre Szervánszky (Hungary, 1911-)	Concerto for Orchestra, "In memoriam Attila József"	Editio Musica Budapest
Alexandre Tansman (Poland, 1897-)	Concerto for Orchestra	M. Eschig, Paris

1955

Robert Blum (Switzerland, 1900-)	Concerto for Orchestra	unpublished
Gösta Nystroem (Sweden, 1890-1966)	Concerto for String Orchestra [No. 2 of 2]	Nordiska, Stockholm
Goffredo Petrassi (Italy, 1904-)	Concerto for Orchestra [No. 5 of 7]	Suvini-Zerboni, Milan

1956

Pavel Blatný (Czechoslovakia, 1931-)	Concerto for Orchestra [No. 1 of 3]	Český Hudebni Fond, Prague
Usko Meriläinen (Finland, 1930-)	Concert for Orchestra	unpublished
Ruben Radica (Yugoslavia, 1931-)	Concerto for Chamber Orchestra	unpublished

1957

Niels Viggo Bentzon (Denmark, 1919-)	Concerto for Strings	W. Hansen, Copenhagen
Pavel Blatný (Czechoslovakia, 1931-)	Concerto for Chamber Orchestra [No. 2 of 3]	Český Hudebni Fond, Prague
Fritz Büchtger (Germany, 1903-)	Concerto for Orchestra	Sirius, Berlin
Dezider Kardoš (Czechoslovakia, 1914-)	Op. 30, Concerto for Orchestra	unpublished
Goffredo Petrassi (Italy, 1904-)	Concerto for Orchestra [No. 6 of 7], "Invenzione concertata," for strings, brass, percussion	Suvini-Zerboni, Milan
Arnold Walter (Czechoslovakia-Canada, 1902-)	Concerto for Orchestra	unpublished

1958

Tudor Ciortea (Rumania, 1903-)	Concerto for String Orchestra	Editura Muzicală, Bucharest
Will Eisma (Holland, 1929-)	Concerto [No. 1 of 3] for Chamber Orchestra	unpublished
George Rochberg (U.S., 1918-)	Cheltenham Concerto for Chamber Orchestra	T. Presser, Bryn Mawr

Carlos Surinach (Spain-U.S., 1915-)	Concerto for Orchestra	G. Ricordi, Milan

1959

Will Eisma (Holland, 1920-)	Concertino for Chamber Orchestra [No. 2 of 3]	Donemus Founda- tion, Amsterdam
Gene Gutchë (Germany-U.S., 1907-)	Op. 28, Concertino for Orchestra	Fleisher Music Collection, Philadelphia
Paavo Heininen (Finland, 1938-)	Concerto for String Orchestra [No. 1 of 2, revised 1963]	unpublished
Benjamin Lees (U.S., 1924-)	Concerto for Orchestra	Boosey and Hawkes, New York
Colin McPhee (Canada, U.S., 1901-1964)	Concerto for Wind Orchestra	C.F. Peters, New York
Quincy Porter (U.S., 1897-1966)	Concerto for Wind Orchestra	C.F. Peters, New York

1960

Will Eisma (Holland, 1929-)	Concerto for Orchestra [No. 3 of 3]	Donemus Founda- tion, Amsterdam
Alberto Bruni Tedeschi (Italy, 1915-)	Concerto for Orchestra [No. 1 of 2]	unpublished

1961

Kenneth Leighton (England, 1929-)	Concerto for Large String Orchestra	Novello, London
Jaan Rääts (U.S.S.R., 1932-)	Op. 16, Concerto for Chamber Orchestra	unpublished
Zeno Vancea (Rumania, 1900-)	Concerto for String Orchestra	Editura Muzicală, Bucharest

1962

Grażyna Bacewicz (Poland, 1913-1969)	Concerto for Orchestra	Polskie Wydawnictwo Muzyczne, Warsaw
Max Butting (Germany, 1888-)	Op. 104, Wochenend Konzert	Internationale Musikbibliothek, East Berlin
Antón García-Abril (Spain, 1933-)	Concerto for String Instruments	Union Musical Española, Madrid
Günter Kochan (Germany, 1930-)	Concerto for Orchestra	Verlag Neue Musik, East Berlin
Alberto Bruni Tedeschi (Italy, 1915-)	Concerto for Orchestra [No. 2 of 2]	unpublished

1962-1963

| Michael Tippett | Concerto for Orchestra | B. Schott, Mainz |
| (England, 1905-) | [No. 2 of 2] | |

1962-1964

| Pavel Blatný | Concerto for Jazz Orchestra | Edition Modern, |
| (Czechoslovakia, 1931-) | [No. 3 of 3] | Munich |

1963

Harald Genzmer	Concerto [No. 2 of 2] for	C.F. Peters,
(Germany, 1909-)	Orchestra	Frankfurt
Paavo Heininen	Adagio: Concerto for Orchestra	unpublished
(Finland, 1938-)	in the Form of Variations	
	[No. 2 of 2, revised 1966]	
Diether de la Motte	Concerto for Orchestra	Bärenreiter, Kassel
(Germany, 1928-)		
Milan Ristić	Concerto for Orchestra	Serbian Academy
(Yugoslavia, 1908-)	[No. 1 of 2]	of Science and Art,
		Belgrade
Rodion Shchedrin	Concerto for Orchestra	Izdatyelstvo
(U.S.S.R., 1932-)	"Ozornye Tchastushky"	Sovyetskii
	["Naughty Folk Tunes"]	Kompozitor, Moscow
Rezső Sugár	Concerto for Orchestra	Editio Musica
(Hungary, 1919-)		Budapest

1964

William Mathias	Concerto for Orchestra	unpublished
(Wales, 1934-)		
Akira Miyoshi	Concerto for Orchestra	Ongaku no
(Japan, 1933-)		Tomo-sha, Tokyo
Goffredo Petrassi	Concerto for Orchestra	Suvini-Zerboni,
(Italy, 1904-)	[No. 7 of 7]	Milan
Guido Santórsola	Concerto for Orchestra	unpublished
(Italy, 1904-)		
William Sydeman	Concerto for Orchestra,	Okra, c/o Seesaw,
(U.S., 1928-)	"Oecumenicus"	New York

1965

Ikuma Dan	Concerto Grosso for String	unpublished
(Japan, 1924-)	Orchestra	
Roberto Gerhard	Concerto for Orchestra	Oxford, London
(Spain-England, 1896-1970)		
Alberto Ginastera	Op. 33, Concerto per Corde	Boosey and
(Argentina, 1916-)		Hawkes, New York

1965-1966

Gunther Schuller (U.S., 1925-)	Concerto for Orchestra, "Gala Music"	Associated, New York

1966

Viktor Kalabis (Czechoslovakia, 1923-)	Op. 25, Concerto for Orchestra [No. 2 of 2]	Union of Czechoslovak Composers, Prague
John Tavener (England, 1944-)	Chamber Concerto for Orchestra	J. and W. Chester, London

1967

Andrei Eshpai (U.S.S.R., 1925-)	Concerto for Orchestra	Mezhdunarod- naya Kniga, Moscow
Theodore Karyotakis (Greece, 1903-)	Concerto for Orchestra	unpublished
Robert Hall Lewis (U.S., 1926-)	Concerto for Chamber Orchestra	unpublished
Thea Musgrave (England, 1928-)	Concerto for Orchestra	J. and W. Chester London

1968

Ezra Laderman (U.S., 1924-)	Satire: Concerto for Orchestra	Oxford, London

1969

Elliott Carter (U.S., 1908-)	Concerto for Orchestra	Associated, New York
Milan Ristić (Yugoslavia, 1908-)	Concerto for String Orchestra [No. 2 of 2]	unpublished

1970

Jacques Bondon (France, 1927-)	Concerto for String Orchestra, "Lumières et formes animées"	M. Eschig, Paris

1971

Jurii Falik (U.S.S.R., 1936-)	Concerto for Orchestra (based on the Till Eulenspiegel legends)	Muzyka, Moscow

1972

Samuel H. Adler (Germany-U.S., 1928-)	Concerto for Orchestra	Boosey and Hawkes, New York

1973

Richard Rodney Bennett (England, 1936-)	Concerto for Orchestra	Novello, London

1974

Anthony Payne   Concerto for Orchestra   J. and W. Chester,
(England, 1936-   )   London

April 1973
(revised May 1976)

A Change of Mind

During the first half of this century critics and historians said frequently that we were living in a period of transition. More recently the idea of a transition has subsided and the twentieth century has been thought of as a separate, though highly eclectic, era. Various dates are given to mark the beginning of this period—the year 1900 or World War I, for example— but none of them quite works and there is always much shunting back and forth over the border to explain all the composers who apparently were out of step with their contemporaries. Also troublesome are the stylistic categories generally used: chromaticism, impressionism, nationalism, atonality, dodecaphony, folklorism, microtonalism, dadaism, neoclassicism, serialism, minimalism, indeterminacy, and the like. Some of them refer to harmonic ideas, others to source materials, others to structure, others to philosophy. None of them specifically mentions a central characteristic of our time, the rise of texture and timbre as prime thematic elements. I have yet to read—or write—a neat definition of neoclassicism or

This essay was published in English in *Music Review* (England) 35, nos. 3-4 (November 1974); in Spanish in *Heterofonía* (Mexico) 45 (November 1975); in Polish in *Res Facta* (Poland) 1976; and in Portuguese by the Editora de Escola de Comunicações e Artes of the University of São Paulo, Brazil, 1976.

135

make a clean separation between the music of Schoenberg and that of the neoclassic movement or find a satisfactory niche for such composers as Ives, Bartók, and Carter. Having been more or less taught to accept confusion as inherent in the twentieth century, I never used to question these matters, but now that the avant-garde is claiming kinship with old enemies like Liszt, Wagner, and Mahler, I feel compelled to search for a new perspective on recent music in the West.

Almost everyone will agree that after Beethoven Western music began to change in fundamental ways. This fact is revealed not only by the decline of what theory books call a "common practice" but by the way music history is written. No matter which author one reads, his narrative flows with logic and confidence from the late Middle Ages through Beethoven, and then it changes. Whereas the Gesualdos had been exceptions, odd variations on the musical material that others were using, the Wagners become the rule, struggling for uniqueness and being valued, often as "geniuses," if they achieved it. Consequently, the historical narrative after Beethoven ceases to be a flow and becomes instead a series of whirlpools, first around individual composers and then around isms. Of equal significance is the fact that while historians describe all the changes in style that took place before Beethoven, they rarely ask why they occurred. This would raise the subject of aesthetics, and nothing so radical as a change in the criteria of music was involved before 1800. By contrast the nineteenth century begs an explanation. Although personally I have not found the aesthetics of romanticism satisfying when applied to nineteenth-century music, I am impressed by the fact that the subject is usually discussed. In the twentieth century contemporary music has raised aesthetics to the level of public debate, as can be heard at intermissions when people ask, "Why does it sound like that? What does it mean?"

The public has good reason to be puzzled. Innovative composers have not merely altered a few surface features of style; they have overturned the very system of values upon which Western music is based. Comments like this are often made in jest or derision, but this one is intended to be taken literally, as a statement of historical fact. To make this point clear, I shall outline the processes by which the Western concepts of music disintegrated and the complementary processes by which a different set of ideas took their place. In reality, however, these are not separable. They are the tangled currents of a vast change of mind involving numberless simultaneous and interrelated actions.

Disintegration of the Western System of Music

The disintegration of tonality, one of the two basic components of the Western system of music, is already familiar: A taste for unexpected splashes of harmonic color led composers in the early decades of the nineteenth century to create ever more daring enharmonic and chromatic surprises, and the widespread adoption of equal temperament during these years furthered the cause of harmonic freedom by allowing access to all keys in the major-minor complex, some of which in the preceding systems of temperament had been unpleasantly discordant. Gradually composers and listeners became less concerned about maintaining the pitch hierarchies that produce tonality, and by the 1860s innovative composers were writing such ambiguous chromatic passages that theorists still argue about what key(s) they are in.

The concurrent disintegration of simple metrical rhythm, the other basic component of the Western system of music, is less well understood. Indeed, simple metrical rhythm is so deeply embedded in Western assumptions about music that its role is seldom acknowledged. From the very beginning, however, tonality was welded to this structural principle whose grids of strong and weak beats provided the framework that composers needed to support the intricate harmonic relationships that increasingly fascinated them. The association continued to the end. When harmonic surprises in the form of chromaticism increased during the nineteenth century, rhythmic surprises increased as well. But just as chromaticism at this time always settled back into the tonal system, so did syncopations, hemiolas, meter changes, and polymetric counterpoint tug at the bonds of measured time without ever breaking them. When tonality was occasionally suspended, as in Wagner and Debussy, mensural rhythm was suspended as well. (Though not always apparent in the printed score, the occasional absence of meter, and sometimes of pulse as well, can be heard in performance.)

It should be remembered that the potential for these changes had long existed. The organ preludes of Bach, for example, contain unmetered passages, and some of his chorales incorporate bizarre chromaticisms. Why, then, did a process of disintegration not begin until well into the nineteenth century? The answer lies in the realm of aesthetics and specifically in the models upon which Western music was based. The predominant model of the eighteenth century (I will not speak here of earlier periods) was rhetoric, containing a statement, development, and recapitulation. This required the maintenance of a linear, directional impulse. By contrast the nineteenth century favored the multiple and nondirectional models of nature, poems, stories, and the ebb and flow of emotion. Eventually such composers as Mahler and Ives also explored the private and nonrational regions of freely associated memories. Such models increasingly suggested or required nondirectional pitch relations and, more crucial still, a fluctuating rather than a metered approach to time. The latter is especially clear in the elasticized rhythms of sea and wind in

Debussy and orgasm in Wagner's *Tristan.*[1]

Effects of this change in models are still being felt. Some of the new music around 1900-1910 made no distinction at all between consonance and dissonance in the traditional sense, and shortly thereafter Schoenberg proclaimed that dissonance was "emancipated," meaning, in effect, that for him the hierarchical system of tonality was leveled. After World War II some composers thought of the twelve chromatic pitches less as sounds and more as quantities to be manipulated according to mathematical and other systems. Others abandoned them altogether as a building material in favor of sound and noise collections.

By the turn of the century, the disintegration of metrical rhythm was equally well advanced in the music of innovative composers. Busoni, in a daring leap of mind, drew attention to the rest, the fermata, and "the tense silence between two movements" of a composition. He said that such indeterminate durations most nearly approach the essential nature of music. Schoenberg came close to unmeasured time, perhaps inadvertently, in his atonal works, where the erratic nature of rhythmic impacts unsettles one's perception of the metrical framework. Varèse seems to have aimed more directly at unmeasured time as a necessary adjunct to his juxtapositions of sound masses. In general, however, most composers were reluctant to follow these leads. Until the 1950s the prevailing practice was to retain a simple metrical grid but to distort or disguise it (thus continuing to parallel the practice of tonal harmony). Among the systematic disguises were those by Ives and Partch, who superimposed metrical patterns and timed them

1. The fact that theorists and historians have devoted so much attention to pitch relations in late nineteenth-century music and so little to the concurrent but less visible rhythmic tendencies says much about Western modes of thought. It shows again how long out of practice we are in dealing with the manifold resources of rhythm and how much our understanding of music has come to depend not on what we hear but on what we see on paper.

at different speeds, and Elliott Carter ("metrical modulation," beginning about 1945) and Boris Blacher ("variable meters," beginning about 1950), whose systems facilitate aperiodic successions of beat groupings.

The end of metrical rhythm finally came with serialism (referred to by some writers as "total serialism") and with indeterminacy. In serial writing the durations of pitches and rests were serialized over the time length of a piece, much as pitches had been serialized in 12-tone writing, and this technique pulverized meter just as the earlier one had pulverized tonality. Indeterminacy blocked habitual patterns of rhythmic thought by decreasing a composer's moment-by-moment control over time. Graphic and verbal notations, for example, rarely impose or encourage metrical controls over interior rhythms. The use of unadulterated sounds from the environment, as in Cage's *4'33"*, necessarily results in an unmetered flow. Where the contents of a piece are extremely limited (as in the music of La Monte Young) or densely packed (as in the Cage-Hiller *HPSCHD*), each listener makes his own rhythm by the act of changing the focus of his attention. Many approaches to improvisation since 1950 have created living musical experiences in the sense that the rise and fall of rhythmic energy is the unique, unmetered, on-the-spot interaction of an environment, a few rules, and one or more performers.

Melody, which had leaned heavily on metrical-tonal supports, was one of the first casualties of their disintegration. In Wagner, for example, the fragmentation of line (as in leitmotifs), combined with an avoidance of caesuras, greatly reduced long-range melodic shape and direction. These effects became more pronounced in Debussy, where melody was reduced not only to fragments but to fragments that had no permanent shape. The rise of atonal harmony pulverized melody completely by turning intervals and single pitches into autonomous events. To some extent in 12-tone writing and to a great extent in serialism, the occurrence of a well-shaped melodic line in the old sense is rare and fortuitous. This is also true in Messiaen when he obtains pitch successions by manipulating rhythmic cells. Where texture predominates in today's new music, melodic lines, if they are present at all, are rarely significant; indeterminate procedures have largely prevented their occurrence.

Another casualty of disintegration was (and is) musical notation, which has become troublesome to composers for the first time since the Renaissance. Rhythm began to cause notational problems in the nineteenth century as metrical grids gave way to fluid rhythms that no signs could indicate adequately, not even markings for the newly invented metronome. The solution at that time was to enlarge the vocabulary of verbal directions as to where unmarked rubatos should occur. These solutions, however, have now made the re-creation of nineteenth-century music on its own stylistic terms extremely difficult and perhaps impossible. There is still no precise and easily readable way of telling performers how unmetered time(s) should flow, and the rhythmic notation of even metric composers — including so meticulous a workman as Elliott Carter — often needs considerable editing by publishers before it can be understood by performers. Schoenberg was the first composer since medieval times to have trouble notating pitch. His *Sprechstimme* notation is so ambiguous in this regard that there is serious disagreement today about what he wanted singers to do. The notation of quartertones has been combined successfully with traditional symbols, but smaller divisions of the octave are all but impossible to notate, as are all divisions into nonmultiples of twelve and all divisions not based on the octave. In the case of graphic scores, each piece tends to have a notational system of its own. Already many performers find these scores unintelligible, and unless sufficient recordings are made now as performance guides, they will make little sense to anyone in another half century.

Perhaps the saddest casualty of metrical-tonal disintegration has been the audience for new music. Listeners have not been able to keep up with the growing diversity of alternative structural principles and have largely stopped trying. My friends in college used to play a game that I now realize was made possible by the changing attitude toward structure. We would try to identify famous compositions on the basis of one or two seconds chosen at random from a recording. This proved much easier to do with music written after Beethoven than with music written before, because the usual (but theretofore minor) stylistic differences among composers were so heightened in the nineteenth century that eventually individual pieces came to be based on unique harmonic and textural features. Thus we learned that where structural principles are the common property of many contemporaneous composers, as was the case from the Middle Ages to Beethoven, some unfolding of the structure is needed to make an identification. By contrast, only a momentary sample is needed to identify *Tristan* or *La Mer*. This increasing diversity was, in fact, what caused audience tastes in the nineteenth and twentieth centuries to lag farther and farther behind contemporary developments in composition. Today it would frustrate even an Esterhazy if a "symphony" were announced and he had no idea until he heard the piece what its design and building materials would be. How would he react to a group of serial pieces where each one was based on a system of relationships so complex that it required several pages of description to explain? Or to an indeterminate work where the size, shape, and sound sources might be entirely different the next time he heard it? Or to an evening with La Monte Young where the structure of the sound flow would be in his own perception of it, impossible to share with anyone, including the composer? The profession of music critic came into being partly because people wanted help in dealing with the proliferation of uniqueness, but critics and public alike soon turned to less troublesome issues: They began listening over and over again to familiar pieces and comparing the performances. Alas, the descendants of Nicolas Esterhazy have probably been doing the same.

The Emergence of a New Approach to Music

Obviously, developments over the last 150 years indicate that increasing numbers of composers have found the metrical-tonal system too limiting. In spite of the many historical and personal styles it has been able to accommodate, this system is indeed a severely restricted approach to music. Under its influence composers in the West put the resources of rhythm behind bars and then virtually forgot about them. They rejected most of the world's sounds, including most sounds of the human voice, because they did not reduce to discrete pitches, twelve to the octave. They also rejected countless musical instruments because they were not tuned properly or produced too many subtleties of pitch and articulation. They rejected dissonances that were not closely bound by metrical and tonal controls. They developed taboos against tritones, wolf tones, and other phenomena that threatened the integrity of the system. In short, they rejected everything that did not fit the system or could not easily be adapted to it.

Composers in the nineteenth century began to question the need for all these restrictions, I think, as they became more aware of their own individuality and of the alternate models of form (not based on rhetoric) that they might successfully use. This may have begun as a superficial reaction to the extreme rationality and conformity of the eighteenth century, but the widely varied approaches to structure used later on by Wagner, Debussy, Ives, Scriabin, Schoenberg, and others indicate that the change grew increasingly radical.

Indeed, we now know that it was motivated in part by a fundamental change in attitude toward the nature and purpose of art, namely, that every work should be the unique "self-expression" of its author rather than an instance of some generalized or objectified state of being.[2] Continuing along this path, composers in the twentieth century have searched high and low for new structural ideas: in the nonconcert traditions of their homelands (the European folk musics long forgotten by cultivated musicians), in the musical traditions of other continents (especially Africa and Asia), in the common sounds of daily life, and in nonmusical fields such as linguistics, mathematics, and electronic technology.

Significantly, none of these alternatives has followed the pattern of previous history by dominating the others or joining with them in some new common denominator of structure. Instead they have produced two new concepts in musical composition, *structural multiplicity* and *primacy of sound*. Today the invention of a suitable underlying structure is one of the chief acts of composition (which helps to explain the decreased productivity of composers today as compared with those before Beethoven — and also the "whirlpool" approach to the history of nineteenth- and twentieth-century music). Furthermore, all sounds nowadays, including resources from the metrical-tonal system, are considered potentially musical, and with increasing frequency the structures that composers use have been determined by the unique properties of the sounds they have chosen to work with. A few examples will illustrate: The resonance characteristics of the piano determined the harmonic structure of Elliott Carter's *Piano Sonata*. The innate properties of the chosen series determines the structural properties (what Schoenberg called the "basic shape") of a 12-tone

2. Harold Osborne, *Aesthetics and Art Theory* (New York: E. P. Dutton, 1970), pp. 226-38.

or serial piece. Several pitch systems in just tuning, together with instruments of his own invention, constitute the core of Harry Partch's system of music. The desire to focus on concert-hall noise gave John Cage the frame idea for *4'33"*. The electronic music that David Tudor, Gordon Mumma, and others have devised for the Merce Cunningham Dance Company contains such intimate relationships among sound, sound-producing mechanisms, and underlying structure that it is often impossible to separate them.

Western composers began to show an interest in sound (as opposed to a particular classification of sounds) as soon as they began taking liberties with the metrical-tonal system. This is not revealed in the use of new sound sources but in the way composers used the sources at hand, and in particular by the increased attention they gave to timbre; to novel solo and ensemble effects; to density, chord spacing, register, and other details of texture; and to subtleties of dynamics and articulation. It is the treatment of these features, as much as their unique harmonic characteristics, that enables one to identify some works by Wagner and Debussy almost instantly.

It seems to be a chicken-or-egg situation whether composers first took liberties with the metrical-tonal system and then turned to sound and texture as alternate ways of defining musical shape, or whether they first discovered the pleasure of new sounds and then let go of the metrical-tonal system because it would have inhibited further exploration. Whichever the sequence, the conclusion is the same: The Western system of music and the new interest in sound were incompatible. The choice that innovative composers made was to keep working with sound, and it was probably their continuing experience with sound that eventually made them open to non-Western possibilities. Debussy, for example, said that Javanese gamelan counterpoint surpassed Palestrina, when to others it sounded like an amusing disorder. Ives, whose father trained him to be attentive to sound whether or not it conformed to the metrical-tonal system, heard structure in what others dismissed as inadvertency. Likewise, Bartók's openness enabled him to perceive logic in a folk music that others had dismissed as crude. The increasing momentum of such thinking is well illustrated by the interest in microtones. They are all undesirable by Western standards, yet in the 1920s they were being used by composers in several parts of the Western world, and in most cases independently of each other: in Prague (by Alois Hába), in Budapest (by Bartók), in Berlin (by the circle around Busoni), in Paris (by Ivan Wyschnegradsky), in New York (by Hans Barth and Ives), in Cleveland (by Ernest Bloch), in the American Southwest (by Harry Partch), and in Mexico City (by Julián Carrillo).

Also significant was the increasing musical use of noise, that is, sounds of unfocused or indefinite pitch that by definition lie outside the metrical-tonal system. The mere presence of such sounds is not important, since percussion noises had always been allowed in Western music for rhythmic emphasis. Even such novelties as Wagner's anvils and Strauss's wind and thunder machines were justifiable on the grounds that they occurred within a theatrical or programmatic context. However, the way that composers began to use noise is noteworthy, particularly the thematic significance they gave it within a composition. Debussy was again one of the pioneers. He not only commented on the delicacy of Asian percussion instruments but wrote thematic material for Western percussion (in *Jeux*, for example). Concerts entirely of noise machines, which the futurists were giving in the years around World War I, were considered aberrations at the time, as indeed they are by Western standards. The horns, saws, and airplane propeller in George Antheil's *Ballet mécanique* were regarded by serious musicians mostly as a publicity stunt, and their prominence (visually as well as aurally) is indeed inappropriate in a Western work. Varèse's music was disparaged for similar reasons, yet when a work like *Ionisation* for percussion ensemble appears and the same composer goes on to find aesthetic value in the sound of key clicks on the flute (*Density 21.5*), it is obvious that the standards by which he is being ridiculed have lost validity. By this time, the 1930s, it was not only Varèse who had used sounds of indefinite pitch as thematic material but also such diverse figures as Bartók, Alexander Mossolov, Carl Orff, Harry Partch, John Cage, Amadeo Roldán, and Carlos Chávez. (If tone clusters are included in this classification, then earlier music by Ives and Cowell can be added as well.) There is an appealing irony in this development: Percussionists, whom composers used to value least among musicians, suddenly became highly prized. Not only do many of their instruments produce sounds that are by nature outside the metrical-tonal system, but their schooling is unique in its emphasis on the qualities that a good performance of contemporary music demands — versatility and meticulous attention to ensemble phrasing and balance.

It might be illuminating to speculate here on the sound paths that innovative composers could have taken early in the century if Western civilization, when it rejected so much else, had not permitted a few percussion noises to remain. One possibility is that more composers would have embraced the 12-tone method, which provided the only systematic framework for exploring sound within the pitch vocabulary of the metrical-tonal system. This aspect of the method is little appreciated and ought to be emphasized more in books and history classes if only because the usual approach — seeking appropriate serial numbers for all the notes — draws attention to the least beautiful aspects of 12-tone music. The important questions, the questions that reveal beauty, are the same as the moment-by-moment decisions that the composer made as he worked: Why does this tone have the timbre it does? Why is it in this register? Why is it articulated this way? Why is it given this dynamic level? What significance does its duration have? Why is there a rest here? Looking ahead several decades, one sees how important these questions are, because in serialism timbre, register, dynamics, durations, and modes of articulation were actually singled out for systematic examination and treatment.

Another sound-related possibility that composers might have explored is the thematic use of style. Examples were available early in the century in Mahler and Ives, along with the shaping devices of juxtaposition and collage (for which Varèse, too, provided models). Furthermore, researches in music history were creating an awareness of how varied the sound textures of older instruments and styles can be. However, the potential in such material was not appreciated until much later, the 1960s, when the idea of mixing but not blending became a central technique in mixed-media theater, and historical styles became themes in such works as Henri Pousseur's *Votre Faust*, George Rochberg's *Contra mortem et tempus*, Lukas Foss's *Baroque Variations,* Luciano Berio's *Sinfonia,* and Eric Salzman's *The Nude Paper Sermon.*

During the 1920s and 30s the chief additional manifestations of the interest in sound were the frequent use of nonstandard chamber ensembles and oftentimes a concern for the spatial relationships among sound sources. The instrumentation and stage diagrams of Bartók's *Sonata for Two Pianos and Percussion* and *Music for Strings, Percussion, and Celesta* are prime examples. (Leopold Stokowski's experiments with the makeup and seating of the Philadelphia Orchestra are also noteworthy.)

The compositional attitude that was emerging in these years is perhaps best summed up in Varèse's definition of music (borrowed from the physicist Hoëne Wroñsky): "the corporealization of the intelligence that is in sound." There is an underlying supposition in that phrase about man's relation to the materials of music. If sound has "intelligence," then

it approaches the unknowable complexity of a living phenomenon. To give flesh to an intelligence is not to strain out the
supposed impurities and use the remainder for some pre-
structured purpose, but to give expression to whatever in the
sound is essential to its nature. This is a striking reversal of the
roles so strongly encouraged by Western civilization, for by this
definition the composer is the servant of sound and not its
master.

The Neoclassic Interlude

Many years were to pass before these new ideas showed
signs of eventually dominating musical thought. By the 1930s
radicalism had been overpowered by composers (supported of
course by public taste) who reaffirmed the past, turned to
Western history, and became "neoclassic." How and why this
occurred, just at the threshhold of radical change, are among
the most fascinating questions in twentieth-century music.
In the 1970s we have seen a worldwide conservatism coming
immediately after two decades of intense innovative activity in
every field of thought. Perhaps a similar collective sigh initiated
the years of neoclassicism. Economics must have been important
as well. All the industries of music — concert halls, performing
organizations, touring circuits, instrument manufacturers,
music and textbook publishers, schools, musical journalism —
were geared to serve traditional musical needs. A different idea
of music, if it was to be heard and accepted, would have
required a parallel network of alternative institutions. The Great
Depression and World War II made such a luxury impossible.
For these and doubtless other reasons, the new aesthetic values
lay relatively dormant until after the war, and most composers
used their ingenuity to adapt the surface features of recent
innovations to the standards and goals of the past. In so doing
they reaffirmed tonality and metrical rhythm, both now highly

ornamented, and reused forms from long ago. But they did more than play games with history. So profound was their reaffirmation of the Western tradition that it gave birth to a new genre, the concerto for orchestra, the first new collective expression since the mid-nineteenth century. Another significant development occurred when African music made its first (though diluted) appearance in Western concert halls, largely because the syncopated rhythms of jazz complemented the ornaments of tonality already in use.

Developments since 1950

Because of many newsworthy events that occurred around 1950, that year is being used increasingly to mark the emergence of the musical "avant-garde," meaning the group whose music uses sounds and structures foreign to the Western tradition. The following events can be cited: the first serial compositions of Milton Babbitt, Olivier Messiaen, Pierre Boulez, Karlheinz Stockhausen, and finally the neoclassicists led by Igor Stravinsky; the first *musique concrète* studies of Pierre Schaeffer and Pierre Henry; the first indeterminate works of John Cage and his circle; the founding of Tokyo's Experimental Workshop (*Jikken Kobo*); the death of Stalin, which permitted a relaxation of ideological restrictions on composition in the Communist bloc and the reestablishment of contacts between Eastern Europe and the rest of the world; and the resurgence of prosperity in the industrialized nations, which finally permitted the growth of facilities designed to serve new musical needs (such as the first three studios for electronic music, which were established in Paris, Cologne, and New York). Historians often need markers like 1950 and they will probably continue to use this one, but like all the others it can impede understanding. Nothing fundamentally new happened that year. Rather, a few ideas about musical sound and structure, some of them extending back more than a century, began to be codified in specific techniques and institutions, thereby making tangible the existence of a new conception of music.

Primacy of sound and structural multiplicity were explored in the context of serialism by separating some of the traditional categories of musical sound from each other and serializing them. Along with drawing the attention of composers to some of the ingredients in traditional music, this technique systematically destroyed for them an unwanted legacy of the metrical-tonal system, habitual thinking about the relations among musical elements. This may not have been a conscious aim among serial composers, but it was the effect nevertheless. Surface rhythm, in being serialized and used independently of other elements, ceased being the handmaiden of pitch relations and formal articulations. In treating register the same way, composers broke their habit of assigning to each level of texture the type of pitch and rhythmic motion that had so long been associated with it. Likewise, dynamics were systematically divorced from such traditional jobs as reinforcing melodic shapes and distinguishing among the prominent and subsidiary parts of a texture. Some of the other elements of traditional style were similarly freed from old ties and alignments, with the overall result that surprisingly fresh juxtapositions of sound occurred.

The drastic nature of these operations and their quick acceptance in all the centers of new thinking show how difficult it was to break old habits and how anxious composers were to do so. Yet serial music as a type was never popular with the public, and by the mid-1960s only a few composers cared for it as an exclusive compositional method. One probable reason for the public's dissatisfaction was that Western instruments, for which this music was written, are not capable of so precise a control of dynamics and articulations in all ranges. Consequently, most of the aesthetic values in serial music cannot be appreciated because they cannot be heard, which is ironic considering that serialism represented so genuine and serious an attempt to gain more control over the elements of sound. The problem that ultimately made composers unhappy derives, I think, from the approach that serialism took to structure and shape. The preplanning that goes into a serial work is designed to achieve a unique system of relationships that will produce combinations of sound and silence satisfying to the composer. Each system embodies many self-composing features that make the finished piece largely a revelation in time of its underlying relationships. The shape of the piece tends to be static. It tends not to move or progress toward various goals in the Western manner but to stay in one place, revolving wheel within wheel, revealing its aspects in new combinations and reflections. This is so generally the case that it represents a striking reversal of practice, for in Western music one system is used to produce many shapes, whereas in serial music many systems are used to produce one shape. This concentration on systems was a valuable part of the serial experience because it showed many composers that the underlying structure of a composition was one of the options now open to them. But serialism also turned out to be an exceedingly private experience. The uniqueness of a serial piece — including to a large extent the way in which it is a self-expression of the composer — can be shared only with those few people who have the interest and capacity for detailed structural analysis. Not many composers today can accept that degree of isolation, although there does remain an active group, centered mainly at Princeton University, who are continuing to devise complex systems based on linguistic, mathematical, and other models.

Concurrently with serialism, another new approach to structure was developing under the name of indeterminacy. Using this approach composers devised structures not for pieces but for performances. It is significant that many neoclassicists eventually embraced serialism but not indeterminacy, because the former was by far the more traditional. It not only used the pitch and timbral vocabulary of the metrical-tonal system but, more important, operated under the Western aesthetic tenets that works of art should have a permanent shape over which their creator is the ultimate authority. Indeterminacy placed no restrictions on sound and openly questioned the Western emphasis both on permanency and on composer control. The first traces of these ideas date back to the nineteenth century, when composers balked slightly at traditional controls by turning away from the uniquely human model of form, rhetoric, and toward nonhuman models such as nature, or nonrational models such as the flow of emotions and memories. The nineteenth century also devalued permanency and composer control slightly when it encouraged virtuosos to give the music they performed unique interpretations and thus become co-creative personalities. Furthermore, in tolerating innovations that weakened tonality and metrical rhythm, it attacked in a subtle way the scope and standards of traditional control.

John Cage is generally credited with having made these attitudes explicit by introducing indeterminacy. His fame obscures the fact that the techniques of indeterminacy had precedents in Ives, Duchamp, Cowell, Grainger, and in futurist and dada performances. It also detracts from the essential contributions that others around him were making at the same time. However, Cage is a born leader and his notoriety is understandable. I can think of no other composer who combines his inventiveness and articulateness with his ability to inspire fresh ideas in other people and his talent for capturing the public attention. Like so many other composers, his basic motivation in 1950 was to enhance the role of sound in music. This had always been important to him, as evidenced, for example, in the prepared piano, which he invented in 1938, and the *Imaginary Landscapes 1-3* (1939-1942), which were the first fully realized compositions involving electronic sound. His new approach, composition by chance, was similar to serialism in that it blocked habitual patterns of thought. As Cage later said, the value in chance is in removing music from human determinants such as taste, training, and memory. It was quickly apparent, however, that Cage had gone much farther than the serialists on the issue of self-expression. He was not just withdrawing it from view but denying it altogether. His first methods used imperfections in the manuscript paper, the throwing of dice, or other extraneous criteria to determine what notes he would write down. A colleague, Morton Feldman, applied indeterminacy to performance in *Projections* (1950-1951), which uses a proportional notation to indicate approximate durations and gives registral fields from which the performer chooses pitches. Another colleague, Earle Brown, realized the principle of graphic notation more fully in *December 1952* and created the first modular open-form work, *25 Pages* (1953). Four years later a newer member of the circle, Christian Wolff, began to experiment with structures that facilitate spontaneous interactions among performers. These examples indicate that Cage's circle did not take his views on chance very seriously. They immediately turned away from his denial of self-expression and began to explore a different concept, shared self-expression, which involves the performers as well as the composer and sometimes includes the audience as well. Cage's own music during this period shows that he liked the idea. In *For A String Player*, for example, he tells the performer what motions to make but not what sounds should be produced.[3]

If the history of serialism is any guide, the flexibility

---

3. Nowadays most composers prefer that the word *chance* be used only in connection with pieces composed by means of chance processes, and that *indeterminacy* be used in cases where the piece has built-in features that make the final outcome in performance indeterminate. The term *aleatory* is not generally liked.

shown in these early years may have saved indeterminacy from a narrow existence. Its use now is widespread. As a notational convenience it is often used when an ensemble cluster is desired in a basically traditional work: The range and movement of the texture is notated graphically and the performers fill in the pitches at random, thus saving players and composer alike a lot of unnecessary note chasing. Indeterminate procedures have also been combined with other structural principles, as in the open-form procedures in serial music by Boulez and Stockhausen.

More germane to the original aesthetic of shared self-expression is a recent work of Frederic Rzewski, *Coming Together*, which illustrates both the ingenuity and the intensity of expression that an indeterminate structure can embody. Because indeterminacy is still frequently misrepresented, it is worth looking at Rzewski's piece in some detail. It incorporates the text of a letter from one of the inmates killed by police at New York's Attica State Prison. The written score consists of a single mathematically derived sequence of pitches, 6,272 notes long, that takes about twenty minutes to play. Because only one (short) rhythmic value and only seven different pitches are used, the line is an embodiment of rigidity. A bass instrument (electric guitar is recommended) plays this line at a steady tempo while around and over it other instrumentalists (the number is unspecified) improvise according to the following scheme: Each player, at his own discretion, chooses one of the pitches as it hurtles by on the bass instrument and sustains it for awhile. Then he waits in silence and picks another pitch. Later he begins to take groups of two or three pitches from the ongoing line, playing them somewhat faster now but still slower than the bass. Pitches taken from the line can now be ornamented slightly, and the players may incorporate accents or altered rhythmic values to enliven the flow. However, the bass remains rigid, and the other instruments must always drop what they are doing and rejoin it. This process accumulates with shorter and fewer pauses until, at the end of the work, all instruments are playing in unison. Against this a narrator recites the text. It contains eight sentences that are repeated, with pauses between, according to another rigidly held scheme. The thoughts expressed — including concern for his family — are obviously those of a sensitive man. I was not aware of the mechanics of the piece when I first heard it nor of the use of indeterminacy, but only of the feeling of terror — of the sound of people being swept one by one into a system that would eventually destroy them.[4]

One of the curiosities about indeterminacy in its early New York years is that an example was everywhere in the air but not noticed. It had come from Africa and was melded in the hybrid music of jazz. Cage himself was led to the concept of indeterminacy through the philosophies of Asia, and a likely explanation for his own lack of interest in jazz is that ideas inspire him more than music. Within a decade, however, the influence that jazz was having on innovative composers was at least as great as his own.

The most profound influence that jazz had on Western musical thought — and also the subtlest influence — was in the area of composer control. Since it was a "folk" art, Westerners did not have to worry about whether or not this music had a composer or met any of their other requirements for civilized art. They could just accept it for what it was and for the way it sounded. The general public had never before been able to do this with a music of non-Western origin, but because jazz

---

4. Because many surface features in *Coming Together* sound familiar, the advanced historical position of the piece may not be apparent to everyone who hears it. The work contains both the pitches and the regular pulse of the metrical-tonal system, but the structuring of these elements (as in much jazz since the 1950s) is neither tonal nor metrical. Nor do Rzewski's use of indeterminacy and his invention of a unique system conform with Western aesthetics. The position of many other composers (Steve Reich and Terry Riley, for example) is sometimes misinterpreted because their music has an equally familiar surface ring.

incorporated many Western features—metrical rhythm, tonality, Western instruments—it was accessible. Perhaps the idea in jazz of noncontrol or shared control was inconceivable to Westerners in the first half of this century. Or perhaps it was taken as a sign of cultural inferiority; this, at least, would help explain why so-called "good music" radio stations have only recently begun to broadcast jazz. When band leaders like Duke Ellington, Paul Whiteman, and Benny Goodman edited the style for polite society, they were quick to impose control by making their "own" arrangements and going through the charade of pretending to conduct them. Concert composers like Stravinsky, Milhaud, and Copland furthered the impression that jazz was unusual but not un-Western when they too composed it, using its surface features in Western symphonies and concertos. However, a few musicians, mostly poor and mostly black, kept the original aesthetic alive so that eventually it was familiar to all, though not necessarily articulated: Music can be a performance created by a group of people improvising together. It is worth noting that improvisation in the Western tradition had always maintained the concept of a person in charge by being restricted to solos. So foreign is the jazz idea of collective improvisation that some in the professional musical community have not grasped it yet. A newspaper or magazine, for example, often has its "jazz" critic writing opinions about the performances he has heard while the "music" critic is still saying he cannot evaluate a new work because so much depends on what the performers do.

If jazz in its early decades was a poor and exploited stepchild, in the 1950s it became a leader oftentimes more expressive of new aesthetic trends than most avant-garde concert works. As early as the 1940s Charlie Parker had created an experimental jazz, not intended for dancing, that contained irregular, nonmelodic jabs and slashes of sound. In the late 1950s John Coltrane and, later, Ornette Coleman abandoned completely the Western trappings of tonality, meter, and melody, creating a music of improvised sound textures. Though many other jazz instrumentalists were involved in this movement, it is significant that the leaders played saxophone, because this instrument can produce a unique variety of shrieking, wailing, grumbling, and other sounds of indefinite pitch. In the 1960s, jazz of this type was a chief incentive for shared self-expression and collective improvisation in the concert field. In fact, this new jazz, together with the emergence of rock, brought the sounds and shapes of popular and innovative concert musics closer together than at any period since the lifetime of Beethoven.

The reconsolidation of music at several social and intellectual levels was one of the most striking phenomena of the 1960s. Other signs of reintegration in musical culture had long been in evidence. One of them was the resurgence of music theory as an active force in contemporary thought. Theorists, that is, specialists in theory, had caused nineteenth- and early twentieth-century writings on the subject to become stuck in explanations of the Western system and in attempts to justify recent innovations in terms of that system. With Busoni, Ives, Schoenberg, Cowell, Bartók, Hába, Carrillo, Partch, Cage, Babbitt, Xenakis, Young, and many others, composers reestablished theory as a spearhead of new music. An even more striking integrative phenomenon was the invention and development of electronic instruments, the only new idea in the production and control of musical sound since the beginning of recorded history. Here too there were contributions from many segments of society: from scientists and engineers beginning in the nineteenth century, from concert composers beginning early in the twentieth century, from Hollywood film studios (where microphones first were a factor in composition), from dance bands (where microphones first were used in live performance), from radio stations and universities (who built the first studios for electronic music), from various industries (which loaned their electronic facilities and sponsored world's fair pavilions as showcases for electronic works), and from rock bands (who first applied nontaped electronic resources to live performance).[5]

The aesthetic motivations behind the uses of electronic apparatus are perhaps most clearly revealed in those criticisms, based on Western standards of control, that acknowledge the presence of interesting sounds in electronic music but find fault in the simplicity of shapes. Composers agree that in the 1950s simplicity was not always a matter of choice on their part, because the process of building up the sounds in a tape work was extremely cumbersome; the use of computers to control studio equipment and the development of sound synthesizers have reduced that problem. But the main question then and now is aesthetics: Is it the sound that is most important or the use that is made of the sound? If the latter, then there must be evidence of a strong hand at work; if the former, then a simple shape—a curve, an intersecting of planes, a process that reaches its conclusion, a static field—may be the only evidence of human control that is desired outside of the original choice of materials. Electronic devices have multiplied a thousandfold the sounds and structures now possible in music. If shape were as important a consideration in our time, electronic technology would have been applied to extending its variety and complexity as well.

Implications for the History of Western Civilization

After a century and a half of often bewildering innovation, I believe we have reached a plateau from which the aesthetic outlook is not likely to change for a long while. This evaluation agrees both with those people who used to say we were living in

5. A chronology of many of these developments is given in Lowell Cross, "Electronic Music, 1948-1953," *Perspectives of New Music*, 7, no. 1 (1968): 32-65.

a period of transition and with those who now imply that we are living again in a more stable era. However, I think more can be said than this. Many signs also point to the conclusion that we have been witness to one of the most awesome of historical events, a change in civilizations.

The possibility that this might be true has been talked about for several decades. Thinkers from Spengler and Toynbee to Darcy Ribeira and Jonas Salk have pictured Western civilization on the decline, and close observers of political and social developments have been documenting the ever-widening differences between the circumstances of life today and what they were a few generations ago.[6] In 1963 Leonard Meyer went so far as to observe that "underlying this new esthetic [of indeterminacy] is a conception of man and the universe which is almost the opposite of the view that has dominated Western thought since its beginnings."[7] It should not be surprising that a thoughtful musician like Meyer is among the heralds of a new world order. To some extent all of the arts embody the inner feelings and underlying attitudes of people, but in the present case music may well offer the easiest access to such information. Where radical differences can be compared, as is the case now, the abstract nature of music can permit immediate éntree into the human mind, its goals and values, and into the collective mind of a civilization. Thus historians who work with music have the tools to see now what others will be able to deduce only much later, after the ponderous twitching of changing social and political institutions has subsided. Also now, with the benefit

6. Examples of such information are contained in the newsletters of many foundations, especially the Ford and Rockefeller Foundations; in early publications of the Center for the Study of Democratic Institutions (Santa Barbara, Calif., 1967-   ); in Paul Bohannan, "Beyond Civilization," Natural History 80, no. 2 (February 1971), pp. 50-67; in Charles A. Reich, The Greening of America, paperback ed. (New York: Bantam Books, 1970); and in Alvin Toffler, Future Shock, paperback ed. (New York: Bantam Books, 1970).

7. Leonard B. Meyer, "The End of the Renaissance?" Hudson Review 16 (1963): 174.

of hindsight, historians of music can see that the present change has contradicted the expectations of most other observers: It did not involve annihilation but transformation, and it was not abrupt but gradual.

A look at where new popular and concert musics are being listened to and composed shows that the new civilization is not bounded, as were all others in the past, by geography, language, nationality, or race. It consists instead of people the world over whose outlook is conditioned by a high level of education, technology, and contact with the world at large. Thus, although it grew out of the Western scientific and industrial revolutions, it is absorbing the developing countries everywhere, beginning with their technologically or internationally oriented professionals and their university populations. Soon much of China will be an active participant, as most of Japan is today. So unprecedented is this condition in world history that it has yet to be given a satisfactory name. Possibilities such as "contemporary" civilization or "technetronic," "multilateral," "universal," and "post-industrial," to mention a few of the terms I have seen, all sound weak or modish. Indeed, we may have entered an era that overreaches the very concept of *civilization*.

Even so short a distance as now separates us from the mainstream of Western music enables a more detached and more comprehensive view of it than has been possible before. For me, the cultural significance of the metrical-tonal system is revealed with particuliar clarity. I am struck by the fact that it was truly the product of a civilization and not of a single time, person, or group. Since at least the early years of the Renaissance, that particular civilization valued intelligence and courage above all other human qualities and gave its greatest rewards to the products of those qualities, discovery and conquest (both intellectual and geographical). Frequently in real life this dynamism has raged out of control, but in music it was always carefully channeled within the metrical-tonal system. So perfectly does this system embody both the ambitions and the conscience of Western man that it must rank as one of his most sublime creations. No wonder that for centuries it wielded an enviable power. Under its influence men and women in all the Western lands willingly accepted austerity and regimentation. Acting together they rejected most of the world's musical possibilities and refined the remainder until it approached a crystalline essence. This was the kind of unity and discipline that leaders of church and state all wanted to inspire but never could, and we hear the legacy of it today when music is called a "universal language" and promoted in schools because it "builds character."

If we look at rhythm alone, other values come to light. The Western application of simple grids is an epitome of rational thinking, based apparently on those rhythms in man's life which are relatively ordered and directional, such as walking and breathing, to the exclusion of all other possibilities in the universe, including the directionless and indeterminate rhythms of human emotion, pain, and unaided time perception. But the high regard for rational thought, which seems to lie behind these choices, is not the only value that emanates from the grid system. Its overriding emphasis on order and direction also reflects, I feel, an even deeper Western belief, perhaps the deepest one of all, namely, that man's ambition is the measure and purpose of the world.

Today, instead of confining their imaginations within a single structural framework, composers are inventing a myriad of new musical systems. As already noted, this represents a fundamental break with the past. It acknowledges that a myriad of new musical needs and possibilities have come into existence. It may also reflect fundamental changes in the human perception of life: for example, the greater awareness we now have of the world at large and of the differing values of the people who live in it. Even more, it may reflect the vast opportunities we in the new culture have (as compared with almost everyone before the rise of modern technology) to identify and nurture the uniqueness in each of our lives. The new attitude toward rhythm seems to proceed from an equally generous impulse. It does not impose one standard on everything in its path but seeks out the differing values in sounds, in part so that each may exist in its own time.

Most of what I have described suggests that the Western drive for absolute dominion has been replaced in composition by gentler ideas. It would be comforting to believe that social and political institutions could make an equally graceful transition to new goals, but world events prove otherwise. It is, in fact, the inability of old-line leaders to accept the multiplicity of loyalties and desires among the world's peoples that causes most of the blunders and cruelties we hear about and see daily. Within the industries of music a similar reluctance to accept the new world has caused splendid opportunities to be wasted. In the last decade we have seen immense resources in the United States diverted to the building of performing arts centers, centers whose raison d'être is to perpetuate the cultural past and whose interior and exterior architecture collides with contemporary music, theater, and dance; already the audience for what these centers offer is dwindling. We have seen the Ford Foundation channel almost a billion dollars into American orchestras, although innovative composers no longer need them, although listeners no longer can provide enough support for them, although recordings duplicate what orchestras most want to offer; the Foundation now admits that its program has failed and that the orchestras it patronized are still close to ruin.[8] We have seen music critics everywhere, but especially in New York,

8. Oona Sullivan, "Special Report: Symphonic Strains (Financial)," Ford Foundation *Letter*, February 1, 1973, pp. 4-5.

ignore the lofts, studios, churches, and galleries where new music is most often performed and then report that our musical life is stagnating. All too many educators are compounding these wastes by planning music curricula in which the entire non-Western world will still be ignored, including the composers of contemporary music.

Because of actions like these, not only in music but in all the professions, few people realize how privileged they are to be alive at this moment. For the unimaginable is happening in our midst: One civilization after another is changing its old way of thinking and moving toward some new and shared alignment of goals, values, and peoples. The issue here is not whether this development is good or bad but, simply, that it is taking place, that it is one of the greatest changes in human history, and that we are all part of it. The new attitudes that have been emerging in the arts may well be among the first signs of a new and global millennium.

May-October 1973

American Orchestral Music in Perspective

In the early years of its history the orchestra was one of the chief media in which composers tried out new ideas. At that time, of course, the orchestra was itself a new idea and consequently an exciting plaything. This vitality, this use of the medium as an instrument of innovation, continued on a widespread basis for well over two centuries — through the generation of Igor Stravinsky. Even such radically innovative composers as Ives and Varèse found the orchestra compatible. The technical features of its instruments required few, if any, compromises in their thinking, and its massiveness may have contributed to their novel conceptions of form, time, and space.

Naturally, composers closer to past traditions — Thomson, Copland, Barber, and others — also felt at home in the medium. Their penchant for tone painting, their search for novel timbral combinations and chord spacings, and their use of nationalist materials all derived from a tradition reaching back more than

This essay was written as jacket notes for a sampler record album, *The Outstanding Contemporary Orchestral Compositions of the United States* (New York: International Music Exchange, 1975).

halfway into the history of orchestral music. This fact, together with the skill of these composers, has produced music that is gratifying to play and to hear. It is among the most frequently performed American music.

At no point along this twentieth-century conservative-radical continuum did new orchestral music require playing techniques that were unacceptable to listeners and performers — at least not during the first half of the century. Nevertheless there were serious and often debilitating listening and performing problems, many of them rhythmic and harmonic but even more of them conceptual: What is the music about? What should one listen for? What liberties and disciplines are required of the performer?

These are new questions in music. Until a century ago people may have asked them about the music of earlier times and foreign places, but they had no need to ask them about the music of their own time and place. We do; and our need to ask them influences music making everywhere. It fragments audiences, splitting them into listening groups that specialize in one or another type of music. And where broad audience support is needed, as is the case with orchestras, it encourages conservatism. It encourages the selection of a musical repertory the underlying structural principles of which have been around for a long enough time for large numbers of people to feel at home with them.

This was true as early as the 1930s. Already at that time a double practice had come into being. The media of solo and chamber music were being used for purposes of adventure while, in general, the larger media of operatic and orchestral music were being used for accepted and "classic" procedures. New orchestral music in those years rarely used timbre and texture as primary thematic materials, nor did it incorporate much in the way of microtones, indeterminacy, nonmetric rhythm, and nondirectional form, all of which were made available to Western composers during the first decade of the century.

To the contrary, the orchestral music of Ruggles, Riegger, Harris, Schuman, and others of the time reaffirmed the underlying aesthetics of past Western music. Thus, although the forms employed by these artists were often nonstandard and one-of-a-kind, there is no question today but that each of those forms evolved from a desire to produce art works with discernible beginnings, middles, and ends. We today are also able to hear the forward thrust of the phrase structure, not always guaranteed by tonality, as in the past, but often by the interweaving of well-shaped lines. Tonality and simple metrical rhythm, the basic structural components of Western music, are both present, though it is true that by the 1930s most composers in this country were searching for nontriadic alternatives to tonal harmony and new disguises for the underlying Western grid of simple metrical rhythm.

Historians in the future will love these years, the 1930s and 40s. Theorists too will be able to spend whole lifetimes analyzing the delicate balance that was achieved between the way music had been in the past and the way it was going to be in the future. Equally fascinating instances of such balance will doubtless be discovered from later decades as well — in the music of Sessions and Carter, for example.

Nowadays 1950 is generally thought of as a benchmark year in music, like 1600 or 1750 or 1800. By the early 1950s critics in New York and elsewhere found themselves going to bizarre events called "concerts." "What silly noise. It's a put-on. It's dada all over again," they said, uncertain what else to say. Radically new types of musical notation appeared. Tape and electronic music matured. "Contemporary" began to replace "modern" as a term for new music.

Another basic fact of the 1950s, 60s, and early 70s is that movements sprang up everywhere for social and political equality—among Jews, blacks, Indians, Italian-Americans, women, Chicanos, homosexuals, poor people, old people. Almost everyone realized that he or she belonged to at least one group whose right to a full human life had been subverted. Equally significant in the 60s was the extent of protests against U.S. involvement in the wars in Indochina. Not for a long time had so many Americans fought and killed each other over a question of morality.

Upheavals like this often stir up new forms and energies in art, as witness Kabuki and Elizabethan drama. In America of the 1950s and 60s there was not only a new type of theater (called Happenings) but a new type of dance (spearheaded by Merce Cunningham), "independent" and "personal" films, new sorts of painting (Abstract Expressionism and other styles), a new potential medium for art (television), and finally great quantities of new music. More remarkable still, though most people felt that society was being torn apart unmercifully, music was coming together again. With the rise of progressive jazz and later of rock, the sounds and shapes of new "popular" and "serious" music grew closer together than they had been at any time since Beethoven.

The full impact of these developments will not be heard on these records. The orchestra in the 1950s and 60s continued, as in the 30s, to be a medium of more conservative expression. The rising costs of added rehearsals, which radical newness demands, was now almost prohibitive. Furthermore, the social and professional pressures against experimentation were—and still are—enormous. Most symphony subscribers are older people who understandably prefer traditional sounds, and most symphony musicians, having spent years perfecting traditional techniques, understandably resent learning to scrape, scratch, gurgle, or whatever else may be required to produce a contemporary texture.

Nevertheless, there are sounds and procedures in the orchestral music of Brown, Cage, Crumb, Foss, Hovhaness, and others that are unmistakably contemporary. First of all there is an emphasis on sound. It occurs more in some pieces than in others, but every composer alive is part of a major historical change, extending back a century and a half, by which timbre and texture have come increasingly into the forefront of primary musical resources. There is also the influence of Asian thinking, leading to nondirectional fields of sound, to a greater use of percussion noises, and to varying degrees of choice in performance. There is the influence of Africa, via blues and jazz, which has reinforced the use of texture as acceptable thematic material, as well as the use of performer choice in shaping the final outcomes of a composition. Most profound of all, there is clear evidence here of structural multiplicity—that is, of the freedom composers now exercise in building their own systems and ultimately their own aesthetics of music. (In the past and in other cultures today there have been differences in style among composers alive at the same time. Where we in the contemporary world differ is in permitting and even demanding differences in basic underlying structure.)

As an observer of the past and present, I am fascinated by the ways that contemporary composers are using the orchestral medium. After all, this conception of a musical ensemble is one of the glories of Western civilization. Yet as I survey the overall directions in contemporary musical composition, I become increasingly aware that the orchestra may be like other classical institutions around the world (including such things as French haute cuisine and Balinese dance): Its integrity and perhaps its existence are being undermined by fundamental changes in outlook and attitude. No matter, it would seem, how many delightful memories the orchestra can bring to a Western mind: the court musicians at Mannheim or the concerts of

Esterhazy and Solomon or the Salle Pleyel (or, for me, the wax-on-marble smell of Severence Hall in Cleveland, where I used to go as child to hear *Peter and the Wolf*).

If you are interested in the future, as I am, you might ask yourself, How many younger composers share these feelings of tradition and veneration that a good orchestra can inspire? I find that I know very few who do. Most of the younger Americans around me don't seem eager to grapple with things from the past. They seem bent on new things and especially on new media. Their minds are exploding with theatrics, sitars, electronics, and much more.

Sometimes we forget that music history is made by composers. Their tastes and their interests are ultimately what count the most. The new interests that composers are pursuing, so many of which are incapable of an orchestral realization, will inevitably affect the tastes of us all, listeners, performers, and patrons alike. Perhaps we should think about this. Perhaps we should pause, and cherish while we may, not only the orchestra as an institution but the music that many of our contemporaries are still writing for it.

October 1974